CONGREGATION FOR CATHOLIC EDUCATION

CONGREGATION FOR THE CLERGY

D0406175

BASIC NORMS FOR THE FORMATION OF PERMANENT DEACONS

DIRECTORY FOR THE MINISTRY AND LIFE OF PERMANENT DEACONS

UNITED STATES CATHOLIC CONFERENCE
WASHINGTON, DC

Publication No. 5-242
United States Catholic Conference
Washington, D.C.
ISBN 1-57455-242-2

Text and format from
LIBRERIA EDITRICE VATICANA
Vatican City

Published in the United States, July 1998

JOINT DECLARATION AND INTRODUCTION

BASIC NORMS
FOR THE FORMATION OF PERMANENT DEACONS

DIRECTORY FOR THE MINISTRY AND LIFE OF PERMANENT DEACONS

CONGREGATION FOR CATHOLIC EDUCATION

CONGREGATION FOR THE CLERGY

JOINT DECLARATION
AND
INTRODUCTION

JOINT DECLARATION

The permanent Diaconate, restored by the Second Vatican Council, in complete continuity with ancient Tradition and the specific decision of the Council of Trent, has flourished in these last decades in many parts of the Church — with promising results, especially for the urgent missionary work of new evangelisation. The Holy See and many Episcopates, in promoting this ecclesial experience, have continually afforded norms and guidelines for the life and formation of deacons. The growth of the permanent Diaconate, however, now gives rise to a need for a certain unity of direction and clarification of concepts, as well as for practical encouragement and more clearly defined pastoral objectives. The total reality of the Diaconate — embracing its fundamental doctrinal vision, discernment of vocation, as well as the life, ministry, spirituality and formation of deacons — calls for a review of the journey thus far made, so as to arrive at a global vision of this grade of Sacred Orders corresponding to the desire and intention of the Second Vatican Council.

Following the publication of the *Ratio fundamentalis institutionis sacerdotalis* on priestly formation and the *Directory on the Ministry and Life of Priests*, the Congregation for Catholic Education and the Congregation for the Clergy, completing the treatment of what pertains to the Diaconate and the Priesthood, the objects of their competence, now wish to devote particular consideration to the subject of the permanent Diaconate. Both Congregations, having consulted the Episcopate throughout the world and numerous experts, discussed the permanent Diaconate at their Plenary Assemblies in November 1995. The Cardinal Members together with the Archbishop and Bishop Members carefully considered the various consultations and numerous submissions made in the matter. As a result, the final texts of the *Ratio fundamentalis institutionis diaconorum permanentium* and the *Directory for the Ministry and Life of Permanent Deacons* were drafted by the two Congregations and faithfully reflect points and proposals from every geographical area represented at the Plenary Assemblies. The work of both Plenaries illustrated convergence on many points and agreement concerning the clear need for greater uniformity in training so as to ensure the pastoral effectiveness of the Sacred Ministry in confronting the challenges which face it on the eve of the Third Millenium. Therefore, both Dicasteries were requested to undertake the drafting of these documents which are published simultaneously and prefaced by a single, comprehensive introduction. The *Ratio fundamentalis institutionis diaconorum permanentium*, prepared by the Congregation for Catholic Education, is intended not only as a guideline for the formation of permanent Deacons but also as a directive of which due account is to be taken by the Episcopal Conferences when preparing their respective "Rationes". As with the *Ratio fundamentalis institutionis sacerdotalis*, the Congregation offers this aid to the various Episcopates to facilitate them in discharging adequately the prescriptions of canon 236 of the Code of Canon Law and to ensure for the Church, unity, earnestness and completeness in the formation of permanent Deacons.

The *Directory for the Ministry and Life of Permanent Deacons*, as in the case of the *Directory on the*

Ministry and Life of Priests, has, together with its hortative character, juridically binding force where its norms "recall disciplinary norms of the Code of Canon Law" or "determine with regard to the manner of applying universal laws of the Church, explicitate their doctrinal basis and inculcate or solicit their faithful observance".[1] In these specific cases, it is to be regarded as a formal, general, executory Decree (cf. canon 32).

While retaining their proper identity and their own specific juridical quality, both of these documents, published with the authority of the respective Dicasteries, mutually reflect and complete each other by virtue of their logical continuity. It is to be hoped that they will be presented, received and applied everywhere in their entirety. The introduction, here conjointly published with these documents, is intended as a reference point and a normative source for both, while remaining an inextricable part of each document.

The introduction restricts itself to the historical and pastoral aspects of the permanent Diaconate, with specific reference to the practical dimension of formation and ministry. The doctrinal reasons for the arguments advanced are drawn from those expressed in the documents of the Second Vatican Council and subsequent Magisterium.

The documents produced here are intended as a response to a widely felt need to clarify and regulate the diversity of approaches adopted in experiments conducted up to now, whether at the level of discernment and training or at that of active ministry and

[1] Cf. PONTIFICAL COUNCIL FOR THE INTERPRETATION OF LEGISLATIVE TEXTS, *Chiarimenti circa il valore vincolante dell'art. 66 del Direttorio per il Ministero e la Vita dei Presbiteri* (22 October 1994), in "Sacrum Ministerium" 2 (1995), p. 263.

ongoing formation. In this way it will be possible to ensure a certain stability of approach which takes account of legitimate plurality and in turn guarantees that indispensable unity, necessary for the success of the ministry of the permanent Diaconate which has been fruitful and which, at the threshold of the Third Millenium, promises to make an important contribution to New Evangelisation.

The directives contained in the following documents pertain to permanent deacons of the secular clergy, although many, with due adaptation, may also to be applied to permanent deacons who are members of institutes of consecrated life or societies of apostolic life.

INTRODUCTION *

I. The Ordained Ministry

1. "In order to shepherd the People of God and to increase its numbers without cease, Christ the Lord set up in the Church a variety of offices which aim at the good of the whole body. The holders of office, who are invested with a sacred power, are, in fact, dedicated to promoting the interests of their brethren, so that all who belong to the People of God, and are consequently endowed with true Christian dignity, may, through their free and well-ordered efforts towards a common goal, attain to salvation".[2]

The Sacrament of Orders "configures the recipient to Christ by a special grace of the Holy Spirit, so that he may serve as Christ's instrument for his Church. By ordination he is enabled to act as a representative of Christ, Head of the Church, in his triple office of priest, prophet and king".[3]

Through the Sacrament of Orders, the mission entrusted by Christ to his Apostles continues to be exercised in the Church until the end of time. It is thus the sacrament of apostolic ministry.[4] The sacramental act of ordination surpasses mere election, des-

---

* This introduction is common both to the "Ratio" and to the "Directory". It should always be included in both documents in the event of their being printed separately.

[2] SECOND VATICAN COUNCIL, *Lumen gentium*, 18.
[3] *Catechism of the Catholic Church*, n. 1581.
[4] Cf. *ibidem*, n. 1536.

ignation or delegation by the community, because it confers a gift of the Holy Spirit enabling the exercise of sacred power which can only come from Christ himself through his Church.[5] "The one sent by the Lord does not speak and act of his own authority, but by virtue of Christ's authority; not as a member of the community but speaking to it in the name of Christ. No one can bestow grace on himself; it must be given and offered. This fact presupposes ministers of grace, authorised and empowered by Christ".[6]

The sacrament of apostolic ministry comprises three degrees. Indeed "the divinely instituted ecclesiastical ministry is exercised in different degrees by those who even from ancient times have been called bishops, priests and deacons".[7]

Together with priests and deacons as their helpers, the bishops have received pastoral charge of the community, and preside in God's stead over the flock of which they are shepherds in as much as they are teachers of doctrine, priests of sacred worship and ministers of pastoral government.[8]

The sacramental nature of ecclesial ministry is such that it has "intrinsically linked...its *character of service*. Entirely dependant on Christ who gives mission and authority, ministers are truly "slaves of Christ" (cf. *Rom.* 1:11), in the image of him who freely took "the form of a slave" for us (cf. *Phil.* 2:7)".[9]

---

[5] Cf. *ibidem*, n. 1538.
[6] *Ibidem*, n. 875.
[7] SECOND VATICAN COUNCIL, *Lumen gentium*, 28.
[8] Cf. *ibidem*, n. 20; *CIC*, canon 375, § 1.
[9] *Catechism of the Catholic Church*, n. 876.

The sacred ministry also has a *collegial form* [10] and a *personal character* [11] by which "sacramental ministry in the Church...is at once a collegial and a personal service, exercised in the name of Christ". [12]

II. The Diaconate

2. The service of deacons in the Church is document-ed from apostolic times. A strong tradition, attested already by St. Ireneus and influencing the liturgy of ordination, sees the origin of the diaconate in the institution of the "seven" mentioned in the Acts of the Apostles (6:1-6). Thus, at the initial grade of sacred hierarchy are deacons, whose ministry has always been greatly esteemed in the Church. [13] St. Paul refers to them and to the bishops in the exordium of his *Epistle to the Philippians* (cf. *Phil* 1:1), while in his first *Epistle to Timothy* he lists the qualities and virtues which they should possess so as to exercise their ministry worthily (cf. *1 Tim* 3:8-13). [14]

Scripture and Tradition

From its outset, patristic literature witnesses to this hierarchical and ministerial structure in the Church, which includes the diaconate. St Ignatius of Antioch [15] considers a Church without bishop, priest or deacon, unthinkable. He underlines that the ministry of deacons is nothing other than "the ministry of Jesus Christ, who

---

[10] Cf. *ibidem*, n. 877.

[11] Cf. *ibidem*, n. 878.

[12] *Ibidem*, n. 879.

[13] Cf. SECOND VATICAN COUNCIL, *Lumen gentium*, 29; PAUL VI, Apostolic Letter *Ad pascendum* (15 August 1972), *AAS* 64 (1972), p. 534.

[14] Moreover, he also describes several of the sixty who collaborated with him as deacons: Timothy (1 *Thes* 3:2), Epophros (*Col* 1:7), Tychicus (*Col* 3:7; *Eph* 6:2).

[15] Cf. *Epistula ad Philadelphenses*, 4; *Epistula ad Smyrnaeos*, 12, 2: *Epistula ad Magnesios*, 6, 1; F. X. FUNK (ed.) *Patres Apostolici*, Tubingae 1901; pp. 266-267; 286-287; 234-235; 244-245.

was with the Father before time began and who appeared at the end of time". They are not deacons of food and drink but ministers of the Church of God. The *Didascalia Apostolorum*,[16] the Fathers of subsequent centuries, the various Councils [17] as well as ecclesiastical praxis [18] all confirm the continuity and development of this revealed datum.

Up to the fifth century the Diaconate flourished in the western Church, but after this period, it experienced, for various reasons, a slow decline which ended in its surviving only as an intermediate stage for candidates preparing for priestly ordination.

The Council of Trent disposed that the permanent Diaconate, as it existed in ancient times, should be restored, in accord with its proper nature, to its original function in the Church.[19] This prescription, however, was not carried into effect.

[16] Cf. *Didascalia Apostolorum* (Syriac), capp. III, XI: A. Vööbus (ed.) *The Didascalia Apostolorum* (Syriac with English translation), CSCO, vol. I, n. 402 (t. 176), pp. 29-30; vol. II, n. 408 (t. 180), pp. 120-129; *Didascalia Apostolorum*, III, 13 (19), 1-7: F. X. Funk (ed.), *Didascalia et Constitutiones Apostolorum*, Paderborn 1906, I, pp. 212-216.

[17] Cf. canons 32 and 33 of the Council of Elvira (300/303): PL 84, 305; canons 16 (15), 18, 21 of the first Council of Arles. CCL, 148, pp. 12-13; canons 15, 16, and 18 of the Council of Nicea: *Conciliorum Oecumenicorum Decreta*, bilingual edition of G. Alberigo, G.L. Dossetti, Cl. Leonardi, P. Prodi, cons. of H. Jedin, ed. Dehoniane, Bologna 1991, pp. 13-15.

[18] In the first period of Christianity, every local Church needed a number of deacons proportionate to her numbers so that they might be known and helped (cf. *Didascalia Apostolorum*, III, 12 (16): F. X. Funk, ed. cit., I, p. 208). In Rome Pope St Fabian (236-250) divided the City into seven zones (or "regiones", later called "diaconiae") in charge of each of which was placed a deacon ("regionarius") for the promotion of charity and assistance to the poor. Analogous diaconal structures were to be found in many cities of the east and west during the third and fourth centuries.

[19] Cf. Council of Trent, Session XXIII, *Decreta de Reformatione*, canon 17: *Conciliorum Oecumenicorum Decreta*, ed. cit., p. 750.

The second Vatican Council established that "it will be possible for the future to restore the diaconate as a proper and permanent rank of the hierarchy....(and confer it) even upon married men, provided they be of more mature age, and also on suitable young men for whom, however, the law of celibacy must remain in force",[20] in accordance with constant tradition. Three reasons lay behind this choice: (i) a desire to enrich the Church with the functions of the diaconate, which otherwise, in many regions, could only be exercised with great difficulty; (ii) the intention of strengthening with the grace of diaconal ordination those who already exercised many of the functions of the Diaconate; (iii) a concern to provide regions, where there was a shortage of clergy, with sacred ministers. Such reasons make clear that the restoration of the permanent Diaconate was in no manner intended to prejudice the meaning, role or flourishing of the ministerial priesthood, which must always be fostered because of its indispensability.

With the Apostolic Letter *Sacrum diaconatus ordinem*[21] of 18 June 1967, Pope Paul VI implemented the recommendations of the Second Vatican Council by determining general norms governing the restoration of the permanent Diaconate in the Latin Church. The Apostolic Constitution *Pontificalis Romani Recognitio*[22] of 18 June 1968 approved the new rite of conferring the Sacred Orders of the Episcopate, the Presbyterate and the Diaconate and determined the matter and form of these sacramental ordinations. Finally, the Apostolic Letter *Ad pascendum*[23] of 15 August 1972 clarified the conditions for the admission and ordination of candidates

---

[20] SECOND VATICAN COUNCIL, Dogmatic Constitution, *Lumen gentium*, 29.
[21] *AAS* 59 (1967), pp. 697-704.
[22] *AAS* 60 (1968), pp. 369-373.
[23] *AAS* 64 (1972), pp. 534-540.

to the diaconate. The essential elements of these norms subsequently passed into the *Code of Canon Law* promulgated by Pope John Paul II on 25 January 1983.[24]

In the wake of this universal legislation, several Episcopal Conferences, with the prior approbation of the Holy See, have restored the permanent Diaconate in their territories and have drawn up complementary norms for its regulation.

III. The Permanent Diaconate

Reasons for its restoration

3. The experience of the Church over several centuries has generated the norm of conferring the priesthood only on those who have already received the Diaconate and exercised it appropriately.[25] The Order of deacons, however, "should not be considered merely a step towards the Priesthood".[26]

"One of the fruits of the Second Vatican Council was the desire to restore the diaconate as a proper and stable rank of the hierarchy".[27] On the basis of the "historical circumstances and pastoral purposes noted by the Council Fathers, the Holy Spirit, protagonist of the Church's life, worked mysteriously to bring about a new and more complete actualization of the hierarchy which traditionally consists of bishops, priests and deacons. In this manner the Christian community was revitalized, configured more closely to that of the Apostles which,

---

[24] Ten canons speak explicitly of permanent deacons: 236; 276, § 2, 3°; 288; 1031, §§ 2-3; 1032, § 3; 1035, § 1; 1037; 1042, 1°; 1050, 3°.

[25] Cf. *CIC*, canon 1031, § 1.

[26] PAUL VI, Apostolic Letter, *Sacrum diaconatus ordinem* (18 June 1968): *AAS* 59 (1967), p. 698.

[27] Cf. SECOND VATICAN COUNCIL, Dogmatic Constitution *Lumen gentium*, 29; Decree *Ad gentes*, 16; Decree *Orientalium Ecclesiarum*, 17; Allocution of JOHN PAUL II of 16 March 1985, n. 1: *Insegnamenti*, VIII, 2 (1985), p. 648.

under the influence of the Paraclete, flourished as the *Acts of the Apostles* [28] testifies.

The permanent Diaconate is an important enrichment for the mission of the Church.[29] Since the *munera* proper to deacons are necessary to the Church's life,[30] it is both convenient and useful, especially in mission territories,[31] that men who are called to a truly diaconal ministry in the Church, whether liturgical or pastoral, charitable or social, "be strengthened by the imposition of hands, which has come down from the Apostles, and more closely united to the altar so as to exercise their ministry more fruitfully through the sacramental grace of the diaconate".[32]

Vatican City, 22 February 1998, Feast of the Chair of Peter.

<table>
<tr><td>**Congregation for Catholic Education**</td><td>**Congregation for the Clergy**</td></tr>
<tr><td>Pio Card. LAGHI
Prefect</td><td>DARÍO Card. CASTRILLÓN HOYOS
Prefect</td></tr>
<tr><td>✠ JOSÉ SARAIVA MARTINS
Titular Archbishop of Tuburnica
Secretary</td><td>✠ CSABA TERNYÁK
Titular Archbishop of Eminenziana
Secretary</td></tr>
</table>

---

[28] Catechesis of JOHN PAUL II at the General Audience of 6 October 1993, n. 5, *Insegnamenti*, XVI, 2 (1993), p. 954.

[29] "A particularly felt need behind the decision to restore the permanent diaconate was that of a greater and more direct presence of sacred ministers in areas such as the family, work, schools etc. as well as in the various ecclesial structures". Catechesis of JOHN PAUL II at the General Audience of 6 October 1993 n. 6, *Insegnamenti*, XVI, 2 (1993), p. 954.

[30] Cf. SECOND VATICAN COUNCIL, Dogmatic Constitution *Lumen gentium*, 29b.

[31] Cf. *ibidem*, Decree *Ad gentes*, 16.

[32] *Ibidem*, Decree *Ad gentes*, 16. Cf. *Catechism of the Catholic Church*, n. 1571.

CONGREGATION FOR CATHOLIC EDUCATION

RATIO FUNDAMENTALIS INSTITUTIONIS DIACONORUM PERMANENTIUM

BASIC NORMS
FOR THE FORMATION
OF PERMANENT DEACONS

INTRODUCTION

1. The paths of formation

1. The first indications about the formation of permanent deacons were given by the Apostolic Letter *Sacrum diaconatus ordinem*.[1]

[1] Cf PAUL VI, Ap. Lett. *Sacrum diaconatus ordinem* (18 June 1967): *AAS* 59 (1967), pp. 697-704. The Apostolic Letter, at Ch. II, which is dedicated to younger candidates, prescribes: "6. Young men who are to be trained for the office of deacon should go to a special institution where they can be tested, trained to live a truly evangelical life, and instructed on how to perform usefully the duties of their future state. 9. The period of preparation for the diaconate as such should run for a period of at least three years. The course of studies should be arranged in such a way that the candidates make orderly and gradual progress toward gaining an understanding of the various duties of the diaconate and toward being able to carry them out effectively. The whole course of studies might well be so planned that in the last year special training will be given in the principal functions to be carried out by the deacon. 10. In addition, there should be practice in teaching the fundamentals of the Christian religion to children and others of the faithful, in teaching people to sing sacred music and lead them in it, in reading the books of Scripture at gatherings of the faithful, in giving talks to the people, in administering those sacraments which deacons may administer, in visiting the sick and, in general, in carrying out the ministries which may be required of them". The same Apostolic Letter, at Chapter III, which is dedicated to older candidates, prescribes: "14. It is desirable for these deacons, too, to acquire a good deal of doctrine, as was said in nos. 8, 9 and 10 above, or at least for them to have the knowledge which the episcopal conference may judge they will need to fulfil their functions properly. They should therefore be admitted to a special institution for a certain length of time in order to

These indications were then taken up and further
refined in the Circular Letter of the Sacred Congregation for Catholic Education of 16 July 1969, *Come è
a conoscenza*, in which were foreseen "different types
of formation" according to the "different types of diaconate" (for celibates, married people, "those destined for mission territories or for countries which
were still developing", those called "to carry out their
function in countries with a certain level of civilisa-
tion and a fairly developed culture"). Regarding doctrinal formation, it was specified that it must be
above that required for a simple catechist and, in
some way, analogous to that of the priest. The material which had to be taken into consideration when
drawing up the programme of studies was then listed.[2]

The subsequent Apostolic Letter *Ad pascendum*
specified that "in regard to the course of theological
studies that are to precede the ordination of permanent deacons, the Episcopal Conferences, according to
the local situation, are competent to issue the appropriate norms and submit them to the Sacred Congregation for Catholic Education for approval".[3]

---

learn all they will have to know to carry out worthily the office of
deacon. 15. But if for some reason this cannot be done, then the
candidate should be entrusted to some priest of outstanding virtue
who will take a special interest in him and teach him, and who will
be able to testify to his maturity and prudence".

[2] The Circular Letter of the Congregation indicated that courses
must take into consideration the study of sacred scripture, dogma,
moral, canon law, liturgy, "technical training, in order to prepare
the candidates for certain activities of the ministry, such as
psychology, catechetical pedagogy, public speaking, sacred song,
organisation of Catholic groups, ecclesiastical administration, keeping up to date the registers of baptism, confirmation, marriage,
deaths, etc.".

[3] PAUL VI, Ap. Lett. *Ad pascendum* (15 August 1972), VII b):
AAS 64 (1972), p. 540.

The new *Code of Canon Law* brought together the essential elements of this norm into canon 236.

2. After about thirty years from the first directives, and with the contribution of subsequent experiences, it has been thought opportune now to draw up the present *Ratio fundamentalis institutionis diaconorum permanentium*. Its purpose is that of providing an instrument for guiding and harmonising, while respecting legitimate diversity, the educational projects drawn up by the Episcopal Conferences and dioceses, which at times vary greatly from one to another.

2. Reference to a sure theology of the diaconate

3. The effectiveness of the formation of permanent deacons depends to a great extent on the theological understanding of the diaconate that underlies it. In fact it offers the co-ordinates for establishing and guiding the formation process and, at the same time, lays down the end to be attained.

The almost total disappearance of the permanent diaconate from the Church of the West for more than a millennium has certainly made it more difficult to understand the profound reality of this ministry. However, it cannot be said for that reason that the theology of the diaconate has no authoritative points of reference, completely at the mercy of different theological opinions. There are points of reference, and they are very clear, even if they need to be developed and deepened. Some of the most important of these will now follow, without, however, any claim to completeness.

4. First of all we must consider the diaconate, like every other Christian identity, from within the Church which is understood as a mystery of Trinitari-

an communion in missionary tension. This is a necessary, even if not the first, reference in the definition of the identity of every ordained minister insofar as its full truth consists in being a specific participation in and representation of the ministry of Christ.[4] This is why the deacon receives the laying on of hands and is sustained by a specific sacramental grace which inserts him into the sacrament of Orders.[5]

Specific conformation to Christ

5. The diaconate is conferred through a special outpouring of the Spirit (*ordination*), which brings about in the one who receives it a specific conformation to Christ, Lord and servant of all. Quoting a text of the *Constitutiones Ecclesiae Aegyptiacae*, *Lumen gentium* (n. 29) defines the laying on of hands on the deacon as being not "ad sacerdotium sed ad ministerium",[6] that is, not for the celebration of the eucharist, but for service. This indication, together with the admonition of Saint Polycarp, also taken up again by *Lumen gentium*, n. 29,[7] outlines the specific theological identity of the deacon: as a participation in the one ecclesiastical ministry, he is a specific sacramental sign, in the Church, of Christ the servant. His role is to "ex-

---

[4] Cf JOHN PAUL II, Post-synodal Ap. Exhort. *Pastores dabo vobis* (25 March 1992), 12: *AAS* 84 (1992), pp. 675-676.

[5] Cf ECUM. COUNCIL VAT. II, Dogm. Const. *Lumen gentium*, 28; 29.

[6] The *Pontificale Romanum – De Ordinatione Episcopi, Presbyterorum et Diaconorum*, Editio typica altera, Typis Polyglottis Vaticanis 1990, p. 101, cites at n. 179 of the "Praenotanda", relative to the ordination of deacons, the expression "in ministerio Episcopi ordinantur" taken from the *Traditio apostolica*, 8 (*SCh*, 11bis, pp. 58-59), as taken from the *Constitutiones Ecclesiae Aegyptiacae* III, 2: F. X. FUNK (ed.), *Didascalia et Constitutiones Apostolorum*, II, Paderbornae 1905, p. 103.

[7] "(They should be) compassionate, industrious, walking according to the truth of the Lord, who was the servant of all" (ST POLYCARP, *Epist. ad Philippenses*, 5, 2: F. X. FUNK [ed.], *Patres Apostolici*, I, Tubingae 1901, pp. 300-302).

press the needs and desires of the Christian communities" and to be "a driving force for service, or *diakonia*",[8] which is an essential part of the mission of the Church.

6. The *matter* of diaconal ordination is the laying on of the hands of the Bishop; the *form* is constituted by the words of the prayer of ordination, which is expressed in the three moments of anamnesis, epiclesis and intercession.[9] The anamnesis (which recounts the history of salvation centred in Christ) goes back to the "levites", recalling worship, and to the "seven" of the *Acts of the Apostles*, recalling charity. The epiclesis invokes the power of the seven gifts of the Spirit so that the ordinand may imitate Christ as "deacon". The intercession is an exhortation to a generous and chaste life.

The "matter" and "form" of the sacrament

The *essential form* of the sacrament is the epiclesis, which consists of the words: "Lord, send forth upon them the Holy Spirit, that they may be strengthened by the gift of your sevenfold grace to carry out faithfully the work of the ministry". The seven gifts originate in a passage of *Isaiah* 11:2, from the fuller version given by the *Septuagint*. These are the gifts of the Spirit given to the Messiah, which are granted to the newly ordained.

7. Insofar as it is a grade of holy orders, the diaconate imprints a character and communicates a specific sacramental grace. The diaconal character is the configurative and distinguishing sign indelibly impressed in the soul, which configures the one ordained to Christ, who made himself the deacon or

Character and specific sacramental grace

---

[8] PAUL VI, Ap. Lett. *Ad pascendum*, Introduction: *l.c.*, pp. 534-538.
[9] Cf *Pontificale Romanum – De Ordinatione Episcopi, Presbyterorum et Diaconorum*, n. 207: *ed. cit.*, pp. 115-122.

servant of all.[10] It brings with it a specific sacramental grace, which is strength, *vigor specialis*, a gift for living the new reality wrought by the sacrament. "With regard to deacons, 'strengthened by sacramental grace they are dedicated to the People of God, in conjunction with the bishop and his body of priests, in the service (*diakonia*) of the liturgy, of the Gospel and of works of charity'".[11] Just as in all sacraments which imprint character, grace has a permanent virtuality. It flowers again and again in the same measure in which it is received and accepted again and again in faith.

Relationship with Bishops and priests

8. In the exercise of their power, deacons, since they share in a lower grade of ecclesiastical ministry, necessarily depend on the Bishops, who have the fullness of the sacrament of orders. In addition, they are placed in a special relationship with the priests, in communion with whom they are called to serve the People of God.[12]

Incardination

From the point of view of discipline, with diaconal ordination, the deacon is incardinated into a particular Church or personal prelature to whose service he has been admitted, or else, as a cleric, into a religious institute of consecrated life or a clerical society of apostolic life.[13] Incardination does not represent something which is more or less accidental, but is characteristically a constant bond of service to a concrete portion of the People of God. This entails ecclesial membership at the juridical, affective and spiritual level and the obligation of ministerial service.

[10] Cf *Catechism of the Catholic Church*, n. 1570.
[11] *Ibidem*, n. 1588.
[12] Cf ECUM. COUNCIL VAT. II, Decr. *Christus Dominus*, 15.
[13] Cf *C.I.C.*, can. 266.

3. The ministry of the deacon in different pastoral contexts

9. The ministry of the deacon is characterised by the exercise of the three *munera* proper to the ordained ministry, according to the specific perspective of *diakonia*.

In reference to the *munus docendi* the deacon is called to proclaim the Scriptures and instruct and exhort the people.[14] This finds expression in the presentation of the Book of the Gospels, foreseen in the rite of ordination itself.[15]

The "munus docendi"

The *munus sanctificandi* of the deacon is expressed in prayer, in the solemn administration of baptism, in the custody and distribution of the Eucharist, in assisting at and blessing marriages, in presiding at the rites of funeral and burial and in the administration of sacramentals.[16] This brings out how the diaconal ministry has its point of departure and arrival in the Eucharist, and cannot be reduced to simple social service.

The "munus sanctificandi"

Finally, the *munus regendi* is exercised in dedication to works of charity and assistance [17] and in the direction of communities or sectors of church life, especially as regards charitable activities. This is the ministry most characteristic of the deacon.

The "munus regendi"

10. As can be seen from original diaconal practice and from conciliar indications, the outlines of the ministerial service inherent in the diaconate are very well defined. However, even if this inherent ministeri-

---

[14] Cf ECUM. COUNCIL VAT. II, Dogm. Const. *Lumen gentium*, 29.
[15] Cf *Pontificale Romanum – De Ordinatione Episcopi, Presbyterorum et Diaconorum*, n. 210: *ed. cit.*, p. 125.
[16] Cf ECUM. COUNCIL VAT. II, Dogm. Const. *Lumen gentium*, 29.
[17] Cf *ibidem*.

al service is one and the same in every case, nevertheless the concrete ways of carrying it out are diverse; these must be suggested, in each case, by the different pastoral situations of the single Churches. In preparing the formation to be imparted, these should obviously be taken into account.

4. Diaconal spirituality

11. The outlines of the specific spirituality of the deacon flow clearly from his theological identity; this spirituality is one of service.

Spirituality of service

The model "par excellence" is Christ the servant, who lived totally at the service of God, for the good of men. He recognised himself as the one announced in the servant of the first song of the *Book of Isaiah* (cf *Lk* 4:18-19), he explicitly qualified his action as diakonia (cf *Mt* 20:28; *Lk* 22:27; *Jn* 13:1-17; *Phil* 2:7-8; *1 Pet* 2:21-25) and he entrusted his disciples to do the same (cf *Jn* 13:34-35; *Lk* 12:37).

The spirituality of service is a spirituality of the whole Church, insofar as the whole Church, in the same way as Mary, is the "handmaid of the Lord" (*Lk* 1:28), at the service of the salvation of the world. And so that the whole Church may better live out this sprituality of service, the Lord gives her a living and personal sign of his very being as servant. In a specific way, this is the spirituality of the deacon. In fact, with sacred ordination, he is constituted a living icon of Christ the servant within the Church. The *Leitmotiv* of his spiritual life will therefore be service; his sanctification will consist in making himself a generous and faithful servant of God and men, especially the poorest and most suffering; his ascetic commitment will be directed towards acquiring those virtues necessary for the exercise of his ministry.

12. Obviously such a spirituality must integrate itself harmoniously, in each case, with the spirituality related to the state of life. Accordingly, the same diaconal spirituality acquires diverse connotations according to whether it be lived by a married man, a widower, a single man, a religious, a consecrated person in the world. Formation must take account of these variations and offer differentiated spiritual paths according to the types of candidates.

Characterisation of the states of life

5. The role of Episcopal Conferences

13. "It is the competence of legitimate assemblies of Bishops or Episcopal Conferences to decide, with the consent of the Supreme Pontiff, whether and where the diaconate is to be established as a permanent rank in the hierarchy for the good of souls".[18]

The *Code of Canon Law* likewise attributes to the Episcopal Conferences the competence to specify, by means of complementary dispositions, the discipline regarding the recitation of the liturgy of the hours,[19] the required age for admission [20] and the formation given; can. 236 is dedicated to this. The canon lays down that it is the Episcopal Conferences, on the basis of local circumstances, which issue the appropriate norms to ensure that candidates for the permanent diaconate, whether young or of a more mature age, whether single or married are "...formed in the spiritual life and appropriately instructed in the fulfilment of the duties proper to that order...".

The competence of the Episcopal Conferences

---

[18] PAUL VI, Ap. Lett. *Sacrum diaconatus ordinem*, I, 1: *l.c.*, p. 699.
[19] Cf *C.I.C.*, can. 276, § 2, 3°.
[20] Cf *ibidem*, can. 1031, § 3.

14. To assist the Episcopal Conferences in preparing a formation which, as well as being attentive to diverse particular situations, will still be in harmony with the universal direction of the Church, the Congregation for Catholic Education has prepared the present *Ratio fundamentalis institutionis diaconorum permanentium*, which is intended as a point of reference for defining the criteria of vocational discernment and the various aspects of formation. This document—by its very nature—establishes only some basic guidelines of a general character, which constitute the norm to which the Episcopal Conferences must make reference for the preparation or eventual perfecting of their respective national *rationes*. In this way the principles and criteria on the basis of which the formation of permanent deacons can be programmed with surety and in harmony with the other Churches shall be illustrated, without stifling the creativity or originality of the particular Churches.

15. In the same way that the Second Vatican Council established for the *rationes institutionis sacerdotalis*,[21] with this document, the Episcopal Conferences which have restored the permanent diaconate are requested to submit their respective *rationes institutionis diaconorum permanentium* for examination and approval by the Holy See. The same will approve them, firstly, *ad experimentum*, and, then for a specified number of years, so as to guarantee periodic revisions.

6. Responsibility of Bishops

Discernment

16. The restoration of the permanent diaconate in a nation does not imply the obligation of restoring it in all its dioceses. The diocesan Bishop will proceed or

---

[21] ECUM. COUNCIL VAT. II, Decr. *Optatam totius*, 1.

not in this regard, after having prudently heard the recommendation of the Council of Priests and, if it exists, the Pastoral Council, and taking account of concrete needs and the specific situation of his particular Church.

If he opts for the restoration of the permanent diaconate, he will take care to promote a suitable catechesis on the subject, both among laity and priests and religious, in such a way that the diaconal ministry may be fully understood. In addition, he will provide for the setting up of the structures necessary for the work of formation and for nominating suitable associates to assist him by being directly responsible for formation, or, according to circumstances, he will commit himself to employing the formation structures of other dioceses, or those of the region or nation.

Suitable catechesis

The Bishop will then take care that, on the basis of the national *ratio* and actual experience, an appropriate rule be drafted and periodically revised.

An appropriate rule

7. The permanent diaconate in institutes of consecrated life and in societies of apostolic life

17. The institution of the permanent diaconate among the members of institutes of consecrated life and societies of apostolic life is regulated by the norms of the Apostolic Letter *Sacrum diaconatus ordinem*. It establishes that "Institution of the permanent diaconate among religious is a right reserved to the Holy See, which alone is competent to examine and approve the votes of general chapters in the matter".[22] The document continues: "Whatever is said...is

Decisions of general chapters

[22] PAUL VI, Ap. Lett. *Sacrum diaconatus ordinem*, VII, 32: *l.c.*, p. 703.

to be understood as applying to the members of other institutes professing the evangelical counsels".[23]

Each institute or society which has obtained the right to re-establish the permanent diaconate assumes the responsibility of guaranteeing the human, spiritual, intellectual and pastoral formation of its candidates. Such an institute or society must commit itself therefore to preparing its own formation programme which incorporates the specific charism and spirituality of the institute or society and, at the same time, is in harmony with the present *Ratio fundamentalis*, especially as regards intellectual and pastoral formation.

The programme of each institute or society should be submitted for examination and approval to the Congregation for Institutes of Consecrated Life and Societies of Apostolic Life or the Congregation for the Evangelization of Peoples and the Congregation for the Oriental Churches for territories where they are competent. The competent Congregation, having obtained the opinion of the Congregation for Catholic Education as regards intellectual formation, will approve it, firstly *ad experimentum*, and then for a specific number of years, so as to guarantee periodic revisions.

---

[23] *Ibidem*, VII, 35: *l.c.*, p. 704.

I

THOSE INVOLVED IN THE FORMATION
OF PERMANENT DEACONS

1. The Church and the Bishop

18. The formation of deacons, like that of other ministers and all the baptised, is a duty which involves the whole Church. Hailed by the Apostle Paul as "the heavenly Jerusalem" and like Mary "our mother" (*Gal* 4:26), "by preaching and baptism she brings forth sons, who are conceived of the Holy Spirit and born of God, to a new and immortal life".[24] And not only this: imitating the motherhood of Mary, she accompanies her children with maternal love and cares for them so that they all may come to the fullness of their vocation.

The Church's care for her children is expressed in the offering of the Word and sacraments, in love and solidarity, in prayer and in the solicitude of the various ministries. However, in this care, which is, so to speak, visible, the care of the Holy Spirit is made present. In fact "the social structure of the Church serves the Spirit of Christ who vivifies it, in the building up of the body",[25] both in its universality and in the singularity of its members.

The Spirit of Christ, the first figure in formation

In the Church's care for her children, the first figure, therefore, is the Spirit of Christ. It is He who

---

[24] ECUM. COUNCIL VAT. II, Dogm. Const. *Lumen gentium*, 64.
[25] *Ibidem*, 8.

calls them, accompanies them and moulds their hearts so that they can recognise his grace and respond generously to it. The Church must be well aware of this *sacramental* relevance of its educational work.

The Bishop (or Major Superior), the one ultimately responsible for formation

19. In the formation of permanent deacons, the first *sign and instrument* of the Spirit of Christ is the proper Bishop (or the competent Major Superior).[26] He is the one ultimately responsible for their discernment and formation.[27] While ordinarily exercising this duty through the assistants who have been chosen, nevertheless he will he commit himself, as far as is possible, to knowing personally those who are preparing for diaconate.

2. Those responsible for formation

20. Those persons who, in dependence upon the Bishop (or competent Major Superior) and in strict collaboration with the diaconal community, have a special responsibility in the formation of candidates for the permanent diaconate are: the director of formation, the tutor (where the number requires it), the spiritual director and the pastor (or the minister to whom the candidate is entrusted for the diaconal placement).

The director of formation

21. The director of formation, nominated by the Bishop (or the competent Major Superior) has the

---

[26] Equivalent to the Diocesan Bishop in this regard are those to whom the following have been entrusted: territorial prelature, territorial abbey, apostolic vicariate, apostolic prefecture and a stably erected apostolic administration (cf *C.I.C.*, cans. 368; 381, § 2) as well as the personal prelature (cf *C.I.C.*, cans. 266, § 1; 295) and the military ordinariate (cf JOHN PAUL II, Apost. Const. *Spirituali militum curae* [21 April 1986], art. I, § 1; art. II, § 1: *AAS* 78 [1986], pp. 482; 483).

[27] Cf *C.I.C.*, cans. 1025; 1029.

task of co-ordinating the different people involved in the formation, of supervising and inspiring the whole work of education in its various dimensions, and of maintaining contacts with the families of married aspirants and candidates and with their communities of origin. In addition, he has the responsibility of presenting to the Bishop (or to the competent Major Superior) the judgement of suitability on aspirants for their admission among the candidates, and on candidates for their promotion to the order of diaconate after having heard the opinion of the other formators,[28] excepting the spiritual director.

Because of his decisive and delicate duties, the director of formation must be chosen with great care. He must be a man of lively faith and a strong ecclesial sense, have had a wide pastoral experience and have given proof of wisdom, balance and capacity for communion; in addition he must have acquired a solid theological and pedagogical competence.

He could be a priest or a deacon and, preferably, not be at the same time also responsible for ordained deacons. In fact, it would be better for this responsibility to remain distinct from that of forming aspirants and candidates.

22. The tutor, designated by the director of formation from among the deacons or priests of proven experience and nominated by the Bishop (or the competent Major Superior), is the direct companion of each aspirant and of each candidate. He is charged with closely following the formation of each one, offering his support and advice for the resolution of any problems which may arise and for helping to   *The tutor*

---

[28] This also includes the director of the specific house of formation, wherever it exists (cf *C.I.C.*, can. 236, 1°).

make personal the various moments of formation. He is also called to collaborate with the director of formation in the programming of the different formational activities and in the preparation of the judgement of suitability to be presented to the Bishop (or the competent Major Superior). According to circumstances, the tutor will be responsible for only one person or for a small group.

The spiritual director

23. The spiritual director is chosen by each aspirant or candidate and must be approved by the Bishop or Major Superior. His task is that of discerning the workings of the Spirit in the soul of those called and, at the same time, of accompanying and supporting their ongoing conversion; he must also give concrete suggestions to help bring about an authentic diaconal spirituality and offer effective incentives for acquiring the associated virtues. Because of all this, aspirants and candidates are invited to entrust themselves for spiritual direction only to priests of proven virtue, equipped with a good theological culture, of profound spiritual experience, of marked pedagogical sense, of strong and refined ministerial sensibility.

The pastor

24. The pastor (or other minister) is chosen by the director of formation in agreement with the other members of the formation team and taking account of the different situations of the candidates. He is called to offer to the one who has been entrusted to him a lively ministerial communion and to introduce him to and accompany him in those pastoral activities which he considers most suitable; he will also be careful to make a periodic check on the work done with the candidate himself and to com-

municate the progress of the placement to the director of formation.

3. Professors

25. The professors contribute in a relevant way to the formation of the future deacons. In fact by teaching the *sacrum depositum* held by the Church, they nourish the faith of the candidates and qualify them to be teachers of the People of God. For that reason they must occupy themselves not only with acquiring the necessary scientific competence and an adequate pedagogical ability, but also with witnessing with their lives to the Truth which they teach. *Scientific competence and witness of life*

In order to harmonise their specific contribution with the other dimensions of formation, it is important that they be willing, depending on circumstances, to collaborate and be open to discussion with the others involved in formation. In this way they will contribute to providing the candidates with a unified formation and help them in the necessary work of synthesis. *Unified formation*

4. The formation community of permanent deacons

26. Aspirants and candidates for the permanent diaconate, naturally constitute a unique context, a distinct ecclesial community which strongly influences the formation process. *A specific ecclesial community*

Those entrusted with the formation must take care that this community be characterised by a profound spirituality, a sense of belonging, a spirit of service and missionary thrust, and have a definite rhythm of meetings and prayer.

The formation community of permanent deacons can thus be for aspirants and candidates for the dia- *A precious support* conate a precious support in the discernment of their vocation, in human growth, in the initiation to the spiritual life, in theological study and pastoral experience.

5. Communities of origin

27. The communities of origin of aspirants and candidates for the diaconate can exercise some influence on their formation.

Family

For younger aspirants and candidates, the family can be an extraordinary help. It must be invited to "...accompany the formative journey with prayer, respect, the good example of the domestic virtues and spiritual and material help, especially in difficult moments... Even in the case of parents or relatives who are indifferent or opposed to the choice of a vocation, a clear and calm facing of the situation and the encouragement which derives from it can be a great help to the deeper and more determined maturing of a...vocation".[29] As far as married aspirants and candidates are concerned, their commitment must be such that their married communion might contribute in a real way to inspiring their formation journey towards the goal of the diaconate.

The parish community

The parish community is called to accompany the path of its member towards the diaconate with the support of prayer and an appropriate catechesis which, while it makes the faithful aware of this ministry, gives to the candidate a strong aid to his vocational discernment.

Other ecclesial groupings

Those other ecclesial groupings from which aspirants and candidates for the diaconate come can also

---

[29] JOHN PAUL II, Post-synodal Ap. Exhort. *Pastores dabo vobis*, 68: l.c., pp. 775-776.

continue to be for them a source of help and support, of light and warmth. However, they must show, at the same time, respect for the ministerial call of their members, not obstructing them, but rather promoting in them the maturing of an authentic diaconal spirituality and readiness.

6. Aspirant and candidate

28. Finally, the man preparing for diaconate "...is a *Self-formation* necessary and irreplaceable agent in his own formation: all formation...is ultimately a self-formation".[30]

Self-formation does not imply isolation, closure to or independence from formators, but responsibility and dynamism in responding with generosity to God's call, valuing to the highest the people and tools which Providence puts at one's disposition.

Self-formation has its root in a firm determination to grow in life according to the Spirit and in conformity with the vocation received, and it is nourished in being humbly open to recognising one's own limitations and one's own gifts.

[30] *Ibidem,* 69: *l.c.,* p. 778.

II

CHARACTERISTICS OF CANDIDATES
FOR THE PERMANENT DIACONATE

Ecclesial discernment

29. "The history of every priestly vocation, as indeed of every Christian vocation, is the history of an *inexpressible dialogue between God and human beings*, between the love of God who calls and the freedom of individuals who respond lovingly to him".[31] However, alongside God's call and the response of individuals, there is another element constitutive to a vocation, particularly a ministerial vocation: the public call of the Church. "Vocari a Deo dicuntur qui a legitimis Ecclesiae ministris vocantur".[32] The expression should not be understood in a predominantly juridical sense, as if it were the authority that calls which determines the vocation, but in a *sacramental* sense, that considers the authority that calls as the sign and instrument for the personal intervention of God, which is realised with the laying on of hands. In this perspective, every proper *election* expresses an *inspiration* and represents a choice of God. The Church's discernment is therefore decisive for the choice of a vocation; how much more so, due to its ecclesial significance, is this true for the choice of a vocation to the ordained ministry.

[31] *Ibidem*, 36: *l.c.*, pp. 715-716.
[32] *Catechismus ex decreto Concilii Tridentini ad Parochos*, pars II, c. 7, n. 3, Turin 1914, p. 288.

This discernment must be conducted on the basis of objective criteria, which treasure the ancient tradition of the Church and take account of present day pastoral needs. For the discernment of vocations to the permanent diaconate, some requirements of a general nature and others responding to the particular state of life of those called should be taken into account.

1. General requirements

30. The first diaconal profile was outlined in the *First Letter of Saint Paul to Timothy*: "Deacons likewise must be serious, not double-tongued, not addicted to much wine, not greedy for gain; they must hold the mystery of the faith with a clear conscience. And let them also be tested first; then if they prove themselves blameless let them serve as deacons...Let deacons be the husband of one wife, and let them manage their children and their households well; for those who serve well as deacons gain a good standing for themselves and also great confidence in the faith which is in Jesus Christ" (*1 Tim* 3:8-10.12-13).

The profile outlined by Saint Paul

The qualities listed by Paul are prevalently human, almost as if to say that deacons could carry out their ministry only if they were acceptable models of humanity. We find echoes of Paul's exhortation in texts of the Apostolic Fathers, especially in the *Didachè* and Saint Polycarp. The *Didachè* urges: "Elect for yourselves therefore bishops and deacons worthy of the Lord, meek men, not lovers of money, honest and proven",[33] and Saint Polycarp counsels: "In like manner should the deacons be blameless before the face of his righteousness, as being the servants of God and Christ, and not of men. They must not be slanderers, double-tongued, or lovers of money, but

The indications of the Fathers of the Church

[33] *Didachè*, 15, 1: F. X. FUNK (ed.), *Patres Apostolici*, I, *o.c.*, pp. 32-35.

temperate in all things, compassionate, industrious, walking according to the truth of the Lord, who was the servant of all".[34]

The requirements of the Code of Canon Law

31. The Church's tradition subsequently finalised and refined the requirements which support the authenticity of a call to the diaconate. These are firstly those which are valid for orders in general: "Only those are to be promoted to orders who...have sound faith, are motivated by the right intention, are endowed with the requisite knowledge, enjoy a good reputation, and have moral probity, proven virtue and the other physical and psychological qualities appropriate to the order to be received".[35]

Human qualities and evangelical virtues necessary for "diakonia"

32. The profile of candidates is then completed with certain specific human qualities and evangelical virtues necessary for *diakonia*. Among the human qualities which should be highlighted are: psychological maturity, capacity for dialogue and communication, sense of responsibility, industriousness, equilibrium and prudence. Particularly important among the evangelical virtues: prayer, Eucharistic and Marian devotion, a humble and strong *sense of the Church*, love for the Church and her mission, spirit of poverty, capacity for obedience and fraternal communion, apostolic zeal, openness to service,[36] charity towards the brothers and sisters.

Active membership within a Christian community

33. In addition, candidates for the diaconate must be active members of a Christian community and already have exercised praiseworthy commitment to the apostolate.

---

[34] St Polycarp, *Epist. ad Philippenses*, 5, 1-2: F. X. Funk (ed.), *Patres Apostolici*, I, *o.c.*, pp. 300-302.

[35] *C.I.C.*, can. 1029. Cf can. 1051, 1°.

[36] Cf Paul VI, Ap. Lett. *Sacrum diaconatus ordinem*, II, 8: *l.c.*, p. 700.

34. They may come from every social grouping and carry out any work or professional activity, providing that it is not, according to the norms of the Church and the prudent judgement of the Bishop, inconsistent with the diaconal state.[37] Furthermore, such activity must be compatible in practice with commitments of formation and the effective exercise of the ministry.

Work or professional activity

35. Regarding the minimum age, the *Code of Canon Law* prescribes that: "the candidate for the permanent diaconate who is not married may be admitted to the diaconate only when he has completed at least his twenty-fifth year; if he is married, not until he has completed at least his thirty-fifth year".[38]

Minimum age

Lastly, candidates must be free of irregularities and impediments.[39]

Irregularities and impediments

---

[37] Cf *C.I.C.*, cans. 285, §§ 1-2; 289; PAUL VI, Ap. Lett. *Sacrum diaconatus ordinem*, III, 17: *l.c.*, p. 701.

[38] *C.I.C.*, can. 1031, § 2. Cf PAUL VI, Ap. Lett. *Sacrum diaconatus ordinem*, II, 5; III, 12: *l.c.*, pp. 699; 700. Can. 1031, § 3 prescribes that "Bishops' Conferences may issue a regulation which requires a later age".

[39] Cf *C.I.C.*, cans. 1040-1042. The irregularities (perpetual impediments) listed by can. 1041 are: 1) any form of *insanity* or other *psychological infirmity*, because of which he is, after experts have been consulted, judged incapable of properly fulfilling the ministry; 2) the offences of *apostasy*, *heresy* or *schism*; 3) *attempted marriage*, even a civil marriage; 4) *wilful homicide* or actually *procured abortion*; 5) *grave mutilation* of self or others, and *attempted suicide*; 6) *illicit completion of acts of order*. The simple impediments, listed by can. 1042, are: 1) the *exercise of an office or administration forbidden to, or inappropriate to, the clerical state*; 2) the *state of being a neophyte* (except when the Ordinary decides otherwise).

2. Requirements related to the candidate's state of life

a) Unmarried

36. "On the basis of Church law, confirmed by the same Ecumenical Council, young men called to the diaconate are obliged to observe the law of celibacy".[40] This is a particularly appropriate law for the sacred ministry, to which those who have received the charism freely submit.

The permanent diaconate, lived in celibacy, gives to the ministry a certain unique emphasis. In fact, the sacramental identification with Christ is placed in the context of the *undivided heart*, that is within the context of a nuptial, exclusive, permanent and total choice of the unique and greatest Love; service of the Church can count on a total availability; the proclamation of the Kingdom is supported by the courageous witness of those who have left even those things most dear to them for the sake of the Kingdom.

b) Married

37. "In the case of married men, care should be taken that only those are promoted to the diaconate who have lived as married men for a number of years and have shown themselves to be capable of running their own homes, and whose wives and children lead a truly Christian life and have good reputations".[41]

Moreover. In addition to stability of family life, married candidates cannot be admitted unless "their

---

[40] PAUL VI, Ap. Lett. *Sacrum diaconatus ordinem*, II, 4: *l.c.*, p. 699.
Cf ECUM. COUNCIL VAT. II, Dogm. Const. *Lumen gentium*, 29.
[41] PAUL VI, Ap. Lett. *Sacrum diaconatus ordinem*, III, 13: *l.c.*, p. 700.

wives not only consent, but also have the Christian moral character and attributes which will neither hinder their husbands' ministry nor be out of keeping with it".[42]

c) *Widowers*

38. "Those who have received the order of deacon, even those who are older, may not, in accordance with traditional Church discipline, enter into marriage".[43] The same principle applies to deacons who have been widowed.[44] They are called to give proof of human and spiritual soundness in their state of life.

Human and spiritual soundness

Moreover, a precondition for accepting widowed candidates is that they have already provided, or have shown that they are capable of providing adequately for, the human and Christian upbringing of their children.

d) *Members of institutes of consecrated life and of societies of apostolic life*

39. Permanent deacons belonging to institutes of consecrated life or to societies of apostolic life[45] are called to enrich their ministry with the particular

Integration of charism and ministry

---

[42] *Ibidem*, III, 11: *l.c.*, p. 700. Cf *C.I.C.*, cans. 1031, § 2; 1050, 3°.

[43] PAUL VI, Ap. Lett. *Sacrum diaconatus ordinem*, III, 16: *l.c.*, p. 701; Ap. Lett. *Ad pascendum*, VI: *l.c.*, p. 539; *C.I.C.*, can. 1087.

[44] The Circular Letter, Prot. n. 263/97 of 6 June 1997, of the Congregation for Divine Worship and the Discipline of the Sacraments envisages that one only of the following conditions be sufficient for obtaining dispensation from the impediment found in can. 1087: the great and proven usefulness of the ministry of the deacon to the diocese to which he belongs; that he has children of such a tender age as to be in need of motherly care; that he has parents or parents in law who are elderly and in need of care.

[45] Cf PAUL VI, Ap. Lett. *Sacrum diaconatus ordinem*, VII, 32-35: *l.c.*, pp. 703-704.

charism which they have received. In fact, their pastoral activity, while being under the jurisdiction of the local Ordinary,[46] is nevertheless characterised by particular traits of their religious or consecrated state of life. They will therefore commit themselves to integrating their religious or consecrated vocation with the ministerial vocation and to offering their special contribution to the mission of the Church.

[46] Cf IDEM, Ap. Lett. *Ecclesiae sanctae* (6 August 1966), I, 25, § 1: *AAS* 58 (1966), p. 770.

III

THE PATH OF FORMATION
TOWARDS THE PERMANENT DIACONATE

1. The presentation of aspirants

40. The decision to undertake the path of diaconal formation can come about either upon the initiative of the aspirant himself or by means of an explicit proposal of the community to which the aspirant belongs. In each case, the decision must be accepted and shared by the community.

The different responsibilities

On behalf of the community, it is the pastor (or the superior in religious houses) who must present to the Bishop (or competent Major Superior) the aspirant to the diaconate. He will do so accompanying the candidacy with an illustration of the motivations which support it and with a *curriculum vitae* and pastoral history of the aspirant.

The Bishop (or competent Major Superior), after having consulted the director of formation and the formation team, will decide whether or not to admit the aspirant to the propaedeutic period.

2. The propaedeutic period

41. With admission among the aspirants to diaconate there begins a propaedeutic period, which must be of an appropriate length. During this period the aspi-

Its purpose

rants will be introduced to a deeper knowledge of theology, of spirituality and of the ministry of deacon and they will be led to a more attentive discernment of their call.

Formators 42. The director of formation is responsible for the propaedeutic period; depending on the cases, he may entrust the aspirants to one or more tutors. It is to be hoped that, where circumstances permit, the aspirants may form their own community, with its own cycle of meetings and prayer which also foresees times in common with the community of candidates.

The director of formation will ensure that each aspirant is accompanied by an approved spiritual director and will make contact with the pastor of each one (or another priest) in order to programme the pastoral placement. In addition, he will make contact with the families of married aspirants to make sure of their openness to accepting, sharing and accompanying the vocation of their relative.

The programme 43. The programme of the propaedeutic period, usually, should not provide school lessons, but rather meetings for prayer, instructions, moments of reflection and comparison directed towards ensuring the objective nature of the vocational discernment, according to a well structured plan.

Even during this period, care should be taken, wherever possible, to involve the wives of the aspirants.

Discernment 44. The aspirants are invited to carry out a free and self conscious discernment, basing it on the requirements necessary for the diaconal ministry, without allowing themselves to be conditioned by personal interests or external pressures of any sort.[47]

At the end of the propaedeutic period, the director of formation, after having consulted the formation team and taking account of all the elements in his possession, will present to the proper Bishop (or competent Major Superior) a declaration which outlines the profile of the aspirants' personalities and also, on request, a judgement of suitability.

For his part, the Bishop (or the competent Major Superior) will enlist among the candidates for the diaconate only those about whom he will have reached a moral certainty of suitability, whether because of personal knowledge or because of information received from the formators.

3. The liturgical rite of admission to candidacy for ordination as deacon

45. Admission to candidacy for ordination as deacon comes about by means of a special liturgical rite, "by which one who aspires to the diaconate or priesthood publicly manifests his will to offer himself to God and the Church, so that he may exercise sacred orders. The Church, accepting this offering, chooses and calls him to prepare himself to receive a sacred order, and in this way he is rightly numbered among candidates for the diaconate".[48]

The significance of the rite

---

[47] Cf *C.I.C.*, can. 1026.
[48] PAUL VI, Ap. Lett. *Ad pascendum*, Introduction; cf I a): *l.c.*, pp. 537-538. Cf *C.I.C.*, can. 1034, § 1. The rite for admission among the candidates for Holy Order is found in the *Pontificale Romanum – De Ordinatione Episcopi, Presbyterorum et Diaconorum*, Appendix, II: *ed. cit.*, pp. 232ff.

<table>
<tr><td>The competent superior</td><td>46. The competent superior for this acceptance is the Bishop himself or, for members of a clerical religious institute of pontifical rite or of a clerical society of apostolic life of pontifical right, the Major Superior.[49]</td></tr>
</table>

The competent superior

46. The competent superior for this acceptance is the Bishop himself or, for members of a clerical religious institute of pontifical rite or of a clerical society of apostolic life of pontifical right, the Major Superior.[49]

Celebration on holy days

47. By reason of its public character and its ecclesial significance, the rite is to be held in proper esteem and celebrated preferably on a feast day. The aspirant is to prepare himself for it by a spiritual retreat.

Request for enrolment among the candidates

48. The liturgical rite of admission must be preceded by a request for enrolment among the candidates, which must be prepared and personally signed by the aspirant himself and accepted in writing by the proper Bishop or Major Superior to whom it is addressed.[50]

Enrolment among the candidates for the diaconate does not constitute any right necessarily to receive diaconal ordination. It is a first official recognition of the positive signs of the vocation to the diaconate, which must be confirmed in the subsequent years of formation.

4. Time of formation

At least three years

49. The formation programme must last at least three years, in addition to the propaedeutic period, for all candidates.[51]

Young candidates

50. The *Code of Canon Law* prescribes that young candidates receive their formation residing "for at least three years in a special house, unless the dioce-

---

[49] Cf *C.I.C.*, cans. 1016; 1019.
[50] Cf *ibidem*, can. 1034, § 1; PAUL VI, Ap. Lett. *Ad pascendum*, I a): *l.c.*, p. 538.
[51] Cf *C.I.C.*, can. 236 and numbers 41-44 of the present *Ratio*.

san Bishop for grave reasons decides otherwise".[52]
"The Bishops of a region—or, where it would be
useful, those of several regions in the same country—should join in establishing a college of this kind,
depending on local circumstances. They should
choose particularly well-fitted men to be in charge of
it and should make clear rules regarding discipline
and studies".[53] Care should be taken that these candidates have good relationships with the deacons of the
diocese to which they belong.

51. For those more mature candidates, whether single *More mature*
or married, the *Code of Canon Law* prescribes that *candidates*
they "prepare for three years in a manner determined
by the Episcopal Conference".[54] Where circumstances
permit, this preparation must be undertaken in the
context of a full participation in the community of
candidates, which will have its own calendar of meetings for prayer and formation and will also foresee
meetings in common with the community of aspirants.

Different ways of organising the formation are
possible for these candidates. Due to work and family
commitments, the most common models foresee formational and scholastic meetings in the evenings, during weekends, at holiday time or with a combination
of the various possibilities. Where geographical factors
might present particular difficulties it will be necessary to consider other models, extending over a
longer time period or making use of modern means
of communication.

[52] *C.I.C.*, can. 236, 1°. Cf PAUL VI, Ap. Lett. *Sacrum diaconatus ordinem*, II, 6: *l.c.*, p. 699.
[53] *Ibidem*, II, 7: *l.c.*, p. 699.
[54] *C.I.C.*, can. 236, 2°.

52. *Candidates from institutes of consecrated life* For candidates belonging to institutes of consecrated life or societies of apostolic life, formation will be carried out according to the directives of the eventual *ratio* of the person's institute or society, or by using the structures of the diocese in which the candidates are to be found.

Personalised formation 53. In the cases in which the above-mentioned ways of formation might not be set up or be impracticable, "then the candidate should be entrusted to some priest of outstanding judgement who will take a special interest in him and teach him, and who will be able to testify to his maturity and prudence. Great care must always be taken that only those who have enough learning and are suitable are enrolled in the sacred order".[55]

54. In all cases the director of formation (or the priest responsible) will check that during the whole time of formation every candidate will maintain his commitment to spiritual direction with his own approved spiritual director. In addition, he will ensure the accompaniment, evaluation and eventual modification of each one's pastoral internship.

55. The formation programme, which will be outlined in general in the next chapter, must integrate in a harmonious manner the different areas of formation (human, spiritual, theological and pastoral), it must be theologically well founded, have a specific pastoral finality and be adapted to local needs and pastoral programmes.

---

[55] PAUL VI, Ap. Lett. *Sacrum diaconatus ordinem*, III, 15: *l.c.*, p. 701.

56. The wives and children of married candidates and the communities to which they belong should also be involved in appropriate ways. In particular, there should be also a specific programme of formation for the wives of candidates, to prepare them for their future mission of accompanying and supporting their husband's ministry.

The involvement of wives and children

5. Conferral of the ministries of lector and acolyte

57. "Before anyone may be promoted to the diaconate, whether permanent or transitory, he must have received the ministries of lector and acolyte, and have exercised them for an appropriate time",[56] so that he may "be better disposed for the future service of the word and the altar".[57] In fact the Church "considers it to be very opportune that both by study and by gradual exercise of the ministry of the word and of the altar, candidates for sacred orders should through intimate contact understand and reflect upon the double aspect of the priestly office. Thus it comes about that the authenticity of the ministry shines out with the greatest effectiveness. In this way the candidates come to sacred orders fully aware of their vocation, 'fervent in spirit, serving the Lord, constant in prayer and aware of the needs of the faithful' (*Rm* 12:11-13)".[58]

The significance of the ministries

The identity of these ministries and their pastoral relevance are illustrated in the Apostolic Letter *Ministeria quaedam*, to which reference should be made.

---

[56] *C.I.C.*, can. 1035, § 1.
[57] PAUL VI, Ap. Lett. *Ad pascendum*, II: *l.c.*, p. 539; Ap. Lett. *Ministeria quaedam* (15 August 1972), XI: *AAS* 64 (1972), p. 533.
[58] IDEM, Ap. Lett. *Ad pascendum*, Introduction: *l.c.*, p. 538.

The request for admission	58. Aspirants to lectorate and acolytate, on the invitation of the director of formation, will make a request for admission, which has been compiled and signed freely, and present it to the Ordinary (the Bishop or Major Superior) who has the authority to accept it.[59] Having accepted the request, the Bishop or Major Superior will proceed to the conferral of the ministries, according to the rite of the *Roman Pontifical*.[60]
The interstices	59. It is appropriate that a certain period of time elapse between the conferring of lectorate and acolytate in such a way that the candidate may exercise the ministry he has received.[61] "Between the conferring of the ministry of acolyte and the diaconate there is to be an interval of at least six months".[62]

6. Diaconate ordination

The declaration and request for admission	60. At the conclusion of the formation journey, the candidate who, in agreement with the director of formation, considers himself to have the necessary prerequisites for ordination, may address to the proper Bishop or competent Major Superior "a declaration written in his own hand and signed by him, in which he attests that he is about to receive the sacred order freely and of his own accord and will devote himself permanently to the ecclesiastical ministry, asking at the same time that he be admitted to receive the order".[63]

[59] Cf IDEM, Ap. Lett. *Ministeria quaedam*, VIII a): *l.c.*, p. 533.
[60] Cf *Pontificale Romanum – De Institutione Lectorum et Acolythorum*, Editio typica, Typis Polyglottis Vaticanis 1972.
[61] Cf PAUL VI, Ap. Lett. *Ministeria quaedam*, X: *l.c.*, p. 533; Ap. Lett. *Ad pascendum*, IV: *l.c.*, p. 539.
[62] *C.I.C.*, can. 1035, § 2.
[63] *Ibidem*, can. 1036. Cf PAUL VI, Ap. Lett. *Ad pascendum*, V: *l.c.*, p. 539.

61. With this request the candidate must enclose the certificate of baptism, of confirmation and of the ministries mentioned in can. 1035, and the certificate of studies duly completed in accordance with can. 1032.[64] If the ordinand to be promoted is married, he must present his marriage certificate and the written consent of his wife.[65]

62. Having received the request of the ordinand, the Bishop (or competent Major Superior) will evaluate his suitability by means of a diligent scrutiny. First of all he will examine the certificate which the director of formation is obliged to present to him "concerning the qualities required in the candidate for the reception of the order, namely sound doctrine, genuine piety, good moral behaviour, fitness for the exercise of the ministry; likewise, after proper investigation, a certificate of the candidate's state of physical and psychological health".[66] "The diocesan Bishop or Major Superior may, in order properly to complete the investigation, use other means which, taking into account the circumstances of time and place, may seem useful, such as testimonial letters, public notices or other sources of information".[67]

After having verified the suitability of a candidate and having been assured that he is aware of the new obligations which he is assuming,[68] the Bishop or competent Major Superior will promote him to the order of the diaconate.

---

[64] Cf *C.I.C.*, can. 1050.
[65] Cf *ibidem*, cans. 1050, 3°; 1031, § 2.
[66] *Ibidem*, can. 1051, 1°.
[67] *Ibidem*, can. 1051, 2°.
[68] Cf *ibidem*, can. 1028. For the obligations which ordinands assume with the diaconate, see canons 273-289. In addition, for married deacons, there is the impediment to contracting new marriages (cf can. 1087).

63. Before ordination, unmarried candidates must assume publicly, in the prescribed rite, the obligation of
celibacy; [69] candidates belonging to an institute of consecrated life or a society of apostolic life who have
taken perpetual vows or other form of definitive commitment in the institute or society are also obliged to
this.[70] All candidates are bound personally, before ordination, to make a profession of faith and an oath
of fidelity, according to the formulae approved by the
Apostolic See, in the presence of the Ordinary of the
place or his delegate.[71]

64. "Each candidate is to be ordained...to the diaconate by his proper Bishop, or with lawful dimissorial letters granted by that Bishop".[72] If the candidate
belongs to a clerical religious institute of pontifical
right or to a clerical society of apostolic life of pontifical right it belongs to the Major Superior to grant
him dimissorial letters.[73]

65. The ordination, carried out according to the
rite of the *Roman Pontifical*,[74] is to be celebrated
during solemn Mass, preferably on a Sunday or
holyday of obligation, and generally in the Cathe-
dral Church.[75] The ordinands prepare themselves

---

[69] Cf *ibidem*, can. 1037; PAUL VI, Ap. Lett. *Ad pascendum*, VI: *l.c.*,
p. 539.

[70] Cf *Pontificale Romanum – De Ordinatione Episcopi, Presbyterorum et
Diaconorum*, n. 177: *ed. cit.*, p. 101.

[71] Cf *C.I.C.*, can. 833, 6°; CONGREGATION FOR THE DOCTRINE OF
THE FAITH, *Professio fidei et Iusiurandum fidelitatis in suscipiendo
officio nomine Ecclesiae exercendo*: AAS 81 (1989), pp. 104-106; 1169.

[72] *C.I.C.*, can. 1015, § 1.

[73] Cf *ibidem*, can. 1019.

[74] *Pontificale Romanum – De Ordinatione Episcopi, Presbyterorum et Diaconorum*, cap. III, *De Ordinatione diaconorum*: *ed. cit.*, pp. 100-142.

[75] Cf *C.I.C.*, cans. 1010-1011.

for it by making "a retreat for at least five days, in a place and in the manner prescribed by the Ordinary".[76] During the rite special attention should be given to the participation of the wives and children of the married ordinands.

---

[76] *Ibidem*, can. 1039.

IV

THE DIMENSIONS OF THE FORMATION
OF PERMANENT DEACONS

1. Human formation

66. The scope of human formation is that of moulding the personality of the sacred ministers in such a way that they become "a bridge and not an obstacle for others in their meeting with Jesus Christ the Redeemer of man".[77] Accordingly they must be educated to acquire and perfect a series of human qualities which will permit them to enjoy the trust of the community, to commit themselves with serenity to the pastoral ministry, to facilitate encounter and dialogue.

Formation in the human virtues

Similar to the indications of *Pastores dabo vobis* for the formation of priests, candidates for the diaconate, too, must be educated "to love the truth, to be loyal, to respect every person, to have a sense of justice, to be true to their word, to be genuinely compassionate, to be men of integrity and, especially, to be balanced in judgement and behaviour".[78]

Capacity to relate to others

67. Of particular importance for deacons, called to be men of communion and service, is the capacity to relate to others. This requires that they be affable, hos-

---

[77] JOHN PAUL II, Post-synodal Ap. Exhort. *Pastores dabo vobis*, 43: *l.c.*, p. 732.
[78] *Ibidem*: *l.c.*, pp. 732-733.

pitable, sincere in their words and heart, prudent and discreet, generous and ready to serve, capable of opening themselves to clear and brotherly relationships, and quick to understand, forgive and console.[79] A candidate who was excessively closed in on himself, cantankerous and incapable of establishing meaningful and serene relationships with others must undergo a profound conversion before setting off with conviction on the path of ministerial service.

68. At the root of the capacity to relate to others is affective maturity, which must be attained with a wide margin of certainty in both celibate and married candidates. Such a maturity presupposes in both types of candidate the discovery of the centrality of love in their own lives and the victorious struggle against their own selfishness. In reality, as Pope John Paul II wrote in the Encyclical *Redemptor hominis*, "man cannot live without love. He remains a being that is incomprehensible for himself, his life is senseless, if love is not revealed to him, if he does not encounter love, if he does not experience it and make it his own, if he does not participate intimately in it".[80] As the Pope explains in *Pastores dabo vobis*, this is a love which involves all the aspects of the person, physical, psychological and spiritual and which therefore demands full dominion over his sexuality, which must become truly and fully personal.[81]

Affective maturity

For celibate candidates, to live love means offering the totality of one's being, of one's energies and readiness, to Christ and the Church. It is a demand-

---

[79] Cf *ibidem*: *l.c.*, p. 733.

[80] IDEM, Encycl. Lett. *Redemptor hominis* (4 March 1979), 10: *AAS* 71 (1979), p. 274.

[81] Cf IDEM, Post-synodal Ap. Exhort. *Pastores dabo vobis*, 44: *l.c.*, p. 734.

ing vocation, which must take into account the inclinations of affectivity and the pressures of instinct and which therefore requires renunciation, vigilance, prayer and fidelity to a precise rule of life. A decisive assistance can come from the presence of true friends, who represent a precious help and a providential support in living out one's own vocation.[82]

For married candidates, to live love means offering themselves to their spouses in a reciprocal belonging, in a total, faithful and indissoluble union, in the likeness of Christ's love for his Church; at the same time it means welcoming children, loving them, educating them and showing forth to the whole Church and society the communion of the family. Today, this vocation is being hard tested by the worrying degradation of certain fundamental values and the exaltation of hedonism and a false conception of liberty. To be lived out in all its fullness, the vocation to family must be nourished by prayer, the liturgy and a daily offering of self.[83]

Training in freedom 69. A pre-condition for an authentic human maturity is training in freedom, which is expressed in obedience to the truth of one's own being. "Thus understood, freedom requires the person to be truly master of himself, determined to fight and overcome the different forms of selfishness and individualism which threaten the life of each one, ready to open out to others, generous in dedication and service to one's neighbour".[84] Training in freedom also includes the education of the moral conscience, which prepares

[82] Cf *ibidem*: *l.c.*, pp. 734-735.
[83] Cf IDEM, Ap. Exhort. *Familiaris consortio* (22 November 1981): *AAS* 74 (1982), pp. 81-191.
[84] IDEM, Post-synodal Ap. Exhort. *Pastores dabo vobis*, 44: *l.c.*, p. 735.

one to listen to the voice of God in the depths of one's heart and to adhere closely to it.

70. These many aspects of human maturity—human qualities, ability to relate, affective maturity, training in freedom and education of the moral conscience—must be considered, taking into account the age and previous formation of the candidates, when planning programmes tailored to the individual. The director of formation and the tutor will contribute in the area of their competence; the spiritual director will take these aspects into consideration and check them during spiritual direction. Encounters and conferences which encourage development and give some incentive to maturity are also of use. Community life—in the various forms in which it can be programmed—will constitute a privileged forum for fraternal checks and correction. In those cases where it may be necessary, in the judgement of the formators, and with the consent of the individual concerned, recourse may be made to a psychological consultation.

Programmes and means

2. Spiritual formation

71. Human formation leads to and finds its completion in spiritual formation, which constitutes the heart and unifying centre of every Christian formation. Its aim is to tend to the development of the new life received in Baptism.

When a candidate begins the path of formation for the diaconate, generally he has already had a certain experience of the spiritual life, such as, recognition of the action of the Spirit, listening to and meditating upon the Word of God, the thirst for prayer, commitment to service of the brothers and sisters, willingness to make sacrifices, the sense of the

Church, apostolic zeal. Also, according to his state of life, he will already have matured a certain defined spirituality: of the family, of consecration in the world or of consecration in the religious life. The spiritual formation of the future deacon, therefore, cannot ignore this experience which he has already had, but must seek to affirm and strengthen it, so as to impress upon it the specific traits of diaconal spirituality.

Discovery of and sharing in the love of Christ the servant

72. The element which most characterises diaconal spirituality is the discovery of and sharing in the love of Christ the servant, who came not to be served but to serve. The candidate must therefore be helped progressively to acquire those attitudes which are specifically diaconal, though not exclusively so, such as simplicity of heart, total giving of self and disinterest for self, humble and helpful love for the brothers and sisters, especially the poorest, the suffering and the most needy, the choice of a life-style of sharing and poverty. Let Mary, the handmaid of the Lord, be present on this journey and be invoked as mother and auxiliatrix in the daily recitation of the Rosary.

The Eucharist

73. The source of this new capacity to love is the Eucharist, which, not by chance, characterises the ministry of the deacon. In fact, service of the poor is the logical consequence of service of the altar. Therefore the candidate will be invited to participate every day, or at least frequently, within the limits of his family and professional commitments, in the celebration of the Eucharist and will be helped to penetrate ever deeper into its mystery. Within the context of this Eucharistic spirituality, care will be taken to give adequate appreciation to the sacrament of Penance.

74. Another characteristic element of diaconal spirituality is the Word of God, of which the deacon is called to be an authoritative preacher, believing what he proclaims, teaching what he believes, living what he teaches.[85] The candidate must therefore learn to know the Word of God ever more deeply and to seek in it constant nourishment for his spiritual life by means of its loving and thorough study and the daily exercise of *lectio divina*. *The Word of God*

75. There should also be an introduction to the meaning of the Prayer of the Church. Indeed praying in the name of the Church and for the Church is part of the ministry of the deacon. This requires a reflection on the uniqueness of Christian prayer and the meaning of the Liturgy of the Hours, but especially a practical initiation into it. To this end, it is important that time be dedicated to this prayer during all meetings of the future deacons. *The Prayer of the Church*

76. Finally, the deacon incarnates the charism of service as a participation in the ministry of the Church. This has important repercussions on his spiritual life, which must be characterised by obedience and fraternal communion. A genuine education in obedience, instead of stifling the gifts received with the grace of ordination, will ensure ecclesial authenticity in the apostolate. Communion with his ordained confreres is also a balm for supporting and encouraging generosity in the ministry. The candidate must therefore be educated to a sense of belonging to the body of ordained ministers, to fraternal collaboration with them and to spiritual sharing. *Obedience*

[85] Cf the presentation of the Book of the Gospels, in *Pontificale Romanum – De Ordinatione Episcopi, Presbyterorum et Diaconorum*, n. 210: *ed. cit.*, p. 125.

77. The means for this formation are monthly retreats and annual spiritual exercises; instructions, to be programmed according to an organic and progressive plan, which takes account of the various stages of the formation; and spiritual accompaniment, which must be constant. It is a particular task of the spiritual director to assist the candidate to discern the signs of his vocation, to place himself in an attitude of ongoing conversion, to bring to maturity the traits proper to the spirituality of the deacon, drawing on the writings of classical spirituality and the example of the saints, and to bring about a balanced synthesis of his state of life, his profession and the ministry.

78. Moreover, provision should be made that wives of married candidates may grow in awareness of their husbands' vocation and their own mission at his side. They are to be invited, therefore, to participate regularly in the spiritual formation meetings.

Appropriate efforts should also be directed towards educating children about the ministry of the deacon.

3. Doctrinal formation

79. Intellectual formation is a necessary dimension of diaconal formation insofar as it offers the deacon a substantial nourishment for his spiritual life and a precious instrument for his ministry. It is particularly urgent today, in the face of the challenge of the new evangelization to which the Church is called at this difficult juncture of the millennium. Religious indifference, obscuring of values, loss of ethical convergence, and cultural pluralism demand that those involved in the ordained ministry have an intellectual formation which is complete and serious.

In the Circular Letter of 1969, *Come è a conoscenza*, the Congregation for Catholic Education invited Episcopal Conferences to prepare a doctrinal formation for candidates to the diaconate which would take account of the different situations, personal and ecclesial, yet at the same time would absolutely exclude "a hurried or superficial preparation, because the duties of the Deacon, as laid down in the Constitution *Lumen gentium* (n. 29) and in the Motu Proprio (n. 22),[86] are of such importance as to demand a formation which is solid and effective".

80. The criteria which must be followed in preparing this formation are:
Criteria

a) necessity for the deacon to be able to explain his faith and bring to maturity a lively ecclesial conscience;

b) attention to his formation for the specific duties of his ministry;

c) importance of acquiring the capacity to read a situation and an adequate inculturation of the Gospel;

d) usefulness of knowing communication techniques and group dynamics, the ability to speak in public, and to be able to give guidance and counsel.

81. Taking account of these criteria, the following contents must be taken into consideration: [87]
Contents

a) introduction to Sacred Scripture and its right interpretation; the theology of the Old and New Testament; the interrelation between Scripture and

---

[86] This refers to the Apostolic Letter of PAUL VI, *Sacrum diaconatus ordinem*, n. 22: *l.c.*, pp. 701-702.
[87] Cf CONGREGATION FOR CATHOLIC EDUCATION, Circ. Lett. *Come è a conoscenza* (16 July 1969), p. 2.

Tradition; the use of Scripture in preaching, catechesis and pastoral activity in general;

b) introduction to the study of the Fathers of the Church and an elementary knowledge of the history of the Church;

c) fundamental theology, with illustration of the sources, topics and methods of theology, presentation of the questions relating to Revelation and the formulation of the relationship between faith and reason, which will enable the future deacons to explain the reasonableness of the faith;

d) dogmatic theology, with its various treatises: Trinity, creation, Christology, ecclesiology and ecumenism, mariology, Christian anthropology, sacraments (especially theology of the ordained ministry), eschatology;

e) Christian morality, in its personal and social dimensions and, in particular, the social doctrine of the Church;

f) spiritual theology;

g) liturgy;

h) canon law.

According to particular situations and needs, the programme of studies will be integrated with other disciplines such as the study of other religions, philosophical questions, a deepening of certain economic and political problems.[88]

Institutes of religious sciences or similar schools
82. For theological formation, use may be made, where possible, of institutes of religious sciences which already exist or of other institutes of theological formation. Where special schools for the theologi-

---

[88] Cf *ibidem*, p. 3.

66

cal formation of deacons must be instituted, this should be done in such a way that the number of hours of lectures and seminars be not less than a thousand in the space of the three years. The fundamental courses at least are to conclude with an examination and, at the end of the three years there is to be a final comprehensive examination.

83. For admission to this programme of formation, a previous basic formation is required; this is to be determined according to the cultural situation of the country.

Basic formation

84. Candidates should be predisposed to continuing their formation after ordination. To this end, they are encouraged to establish a small personal library with a theological-pastoral emphasis and to be open to programmes of ongoing formation.

Ongoing formation

4. Pastoral formation

85. In the wide sense, pastoral formation coincides with spiritual formation: it is formation for an ever greater identification with the diakonia of Christ. This attitude must guide the articulation of the various aspects of formation, integrating them within the unitary perspective of the diaconal vocation, which consists in being a sacrament of Christ, servant of the Father.

In the strict sense, pastoral formation develops by means of a specific theological discipline and a practical internship.

86. This theological discipline is called *pastoral theology*. It is "a scientific reflection on the Church as she is built up daily, by the power of the Spirit, in histo-

"Pastoral theology"

ry; on the Church as the 'universal sacrament of salvation', as a living sign and instrument of the salvation wrought by Christ through the word, the sacraments and the service of charity".[89] The scope of this discipline, therefore, is the presentation of the principles, the criteria and the methods which guide the apostolic-missionary work of the Church in history.

The *pastoral theology* programmed for the deacons will pay particular attention to those *fields* which are eminently diaconal, such as:

a) liturgical praxis: administration of the sacraments and sacramentals, service at the altar;

b) proclamation of the Word in the varied contexts of ministerial service: kerygma, catechesis, preparation for the sacraments, homily;

c) the Church's commitment to social justice and charity;

d) the life of the community, in particular the guidance of family teams, small communities, groups and movements, etc.

Certain technical subjects, which prepare the candidates for specific ministerial activities, can also be useful, such as psychology, catechetical pedagogy, homiletics, sacred music, ecclesiastical administration, information technology, etc.[90]

Practical internship　87. At the same time as (and possibly in relationship with) the teaching of pastoral theology a practical internship should be provided for each candidate, to permit him to meet in the field what he has learned

---

[89] JOHN PAUL II, Post-synodal Ap. Exhort. *Pastores dabo vobis*, 57: *l.c.*, p. 758.

[90] Cf CONGREGATION FOR CATHOLIC EDUCATION, Circ. Lett. *Come è a conoscenza*, p. 3.

in his study. It must be gradual, tailored to the individual and under continual supervision. For the choice of activities, account should be taken of the instituted ministries received, and their exercise should be evaluated.

Care is to be taken that the candidates be actively introduced into the pastoral activity of the diocese and that they have periodic sharing of experiences with deacons already involved in the ministry.

88. In addition, care should be taken that the future deacons develop a strong missionary sensitivity. In fact, they too, in an analogous way to priests, receive with sacred ordination a spiritual gift which prepares them for a universal mission, to the ends of the earth (cf *Acts* 1:8).[91] They are to be helped, therefore, to be strongly aware of their missionary identity and prepared to undertake the proclamation of the truth also to non-Christians, particularly those belonging to their own people. However, neither should the prospect of the mission *ad gentes* be lacking, wherever circumstances require and permit it.

Missionary sensitivity

---

[91] Cf ECUM. COUNCIL VAT. II, Decr. *Presbyterorum ordinis*, 10; Decr. *Ad gentes*, 20.

CONCLUSION

89. The *Didascalia Apostolorum* recommends to the deacons of the first century: "As our Saviour and Master said in the Gospel: *let he who wishes to be great among you, make himself your servant, in the same way as the Son of Man came not to be served but to serve and give his life as a ransom for many*, you deacons must do the same, even if that means giving your life for your brothers and sisters, because of the service which you are bound to fulfil".[92] This invitation is most appropriate also for those who are called today to the diaconate, and urges them to prepare themselves with great dedication for their future ministry.

90. May the Episcopal Conferences and Ordinaries of the whole world, to whom the present document is given, ensure that it becomes an object of attentive reflection in communion with their priests and communities. It will be an important point of reference for those Churches in which the permanent diaconate is a living and active reality; for the others, it will be an effective invitation to appreciate the value of that precious gift of the Spirit which is diaconal service.

---

[92] *Didascalia Apostolorum*, III, 13 (19), 3: F. X. FUNK (ed.), *Didascalia et Constitutiones Apostolorum*, I, *o.c.*, pp. 214-215.

The Supreme Pontiff John Paul II has approved this "Ratio fundamentalis institutionis diaconorum permanentium", and ordered it to be published.

Rome, given at the Offices of the Congregations, 22 February 1998, Feast of the Chair of Peter.

Pɪᴏ Card. Lᴀɢʜɪ
Prefect

✠ Jᴏsé Sᴀʀᴀɪᴠᴀ Mᴀʀᴛɪɴs
Titular Archbishop of Tuburnica
Secretary

71

CONGREGATION FOR THE CLERGY

DIRECTORIUM PRO MINISTERIO ET VITA DIACONORUM PERMANENTIUM

DIRECTORY
FOR THE MINISTRY AND LIFE
OF PERMANENT DEACONS

1

THE JURIDICAL STATUS OF THE DEACON

Sacred Minister

1. The origin of the diaconate is the consecration and mission of Christ, in which the deacon is called to share.[1] Through the imposition of hands and the prayer of consecration, he is constituted a sacred minister and a member of the hierarchy. This condition determines his theological and juridical status in the Church.

Incardination

2. At the time of admission to the diaconate, all candidates shall be required to express clearly in writing their intention to serve the Church[2] for the rest of their lives in a specific territorial or personal circumscription, in an institute of consecrated life or in a society of apostolic life which has the faculty to incardinate.[3] Written acceptance of a request for incardination is reserved to him who has authority to incardinate and determines the candidate's Ordinary.[4]

An ecclesial and ministerial bond

---

[1] Cf. SECOND VATICAN COUNCIL, Dogmatic Constitution *Lumen Gentium*, 28a.
[2] Cf. *CIC*, canon 1034, § 1; PAUL VI, *Ad Pascendum*, I, a: *l.c.*, 538.
[3] Cf. *CIC*, canons 265-266.
[4] Cf. *CIC*, canons 1034, § 1, 1016, 1019; Apostolic Constitution *Spirituali Militum Curae*, VI, §§ 3-4; *CIC*, canon 295, § 1.

75

Incardination is a juridical bond. It has ecclesiological and spiritual significance in as much as it expresses the ministerial dedication of the deacon to the Church.

Deacons of the secular clergy 3.   A deacon already incardinated into one ecclesiastical circumscription may be incardinated into another in accordance with the norm of law.[5] Written authorization must be obtained from both the bishop *a quo* and the bishop *ad quem* in the case of deacons who, for just reasons, wish to exercise their ministry in a diocese other than that into which they were incardinated. Bishops should encourage deacons of their own dioceses who wish to place themselves either permanently or for a specified time period at the service of other particular Churches with a shortage of clergy. They should also support in a particular way those who, after specific and careful preparation, seek to dedicate themselves to the *missio ad gentes*. The terms on which deacons afford such service should be duly regulated by contract and agreed upon by the bishops concerned.[6]

It is a duty incumbent on the bishop to care for the deacons of his diocese with particular solicitude.[7] This is to be discharged either personally or through a priest acting as his delegate. Special pastoral care should always be shown to those in particular difficulties because of personal circumstances.

Deacons incardinated into institutes of consecrated life or societies of apostolic Life 4.   The deacon incardinated into an institute of consecrated life or society of apostolic life shall exercise ministry under the jurisdiction of the bishop in all that pertains to the pastoral ministry, acts of public worship and the apostolate. He is, however, also subject to his own superiors' competence and to the dis-

---

[5] Cf. *CIC*, canons 267-268c § 1.
[6] Cf. *CIC*, canon 271.
[7] Cf. PAUL VI, Apostolic Letter *Sacrum Diaconatus Ordinem*, VI, 30: *l.c.*, 703.

cipline of his community.[8] When a deacon is trans-
ferred to a community in another diocese, the superi-
or shall be obliged to present him to the local Ordinary and obtain permission for him to exercise his
ministry in accordance with the procedures agreed
upon, between the bishop and the superior.

5.   The specific vocation to the permanent Diaconate   *Ordination to*
presupposes the stability of this Order. Hence ordina-   *the Priesthood*
tion to the Priesthood of non-married or widowed
deacons must always be a very rare exception, and
only for special and grave reasons. The decision of
admission to the Order of Presbyters rests with the
diocesan bishop, unless impediments exist which are
reserved to the Holy See.[9] Given the exceptional nature of such cases, the diocesan bishop should consult
the Congregation for Catholic Education with regard
to the intellectual and theological preparation of the
candidate, and also the Congregation for the Clergy
concerning the programme of priestly formation and
the aptitude of the candidate to the priestly ministry.

Sacramental Fraternity

6.   By virtue of their ordination, deacons are united to
each other by a sacramental fraternity. They are all dedicated to the same purpose — building up the Body of
Christ — in union with the Supreme Pontiff [10] and subject to the authority of the bishop. Each deacon should
have a sense of being joined with his fellow deacons in

[8] Cf. *CIC*, canon 678, §§ 1-3; 715; 738; cf. also PAUL VI, Apostolic Letter *Sacrum Diaconatus Ordinem*, VII, 33-35: *l.c.,* 704.
[9] Letter of the SECRETARIAT OF STATE to the Cardinal Prefect of
the Congregation for Divine Worship and the Discipline of the
Sacraments, Prot. N. 122.735, of 3 January 1984.
[10] Cf. SECOND VATICAN COUNCIL, Decree *Christus Dominus*, n. 15;
PAUL VI Apostolic Letter *Sacrum Diaconatus Ordinem*, 23; *l.c.,* 702.

a bond of charity, prayer, obedience to their bishops, ministerial zeal and collaboration.

With the permission of the bishop and in his presence or that of his delegate, it would be opportune for deacons periodically to meet to discuss their ministry, exchange experiences, advance formation and encourage each other in fidelity. Such encounters might also be of interest to candidates to the permanent Diaconate. The local Ordinary should foster a "spirit of communion" among deacons ministering in his diocese and avoid any form of "corporatism" which was a factor in the decline and eventual extinction of the permanent Diaconate in earlier centuries.

Rights and obligations

7.   The Diaconate brings with it a series of rights and duties as foreseen by canons 273-283 of the *Code of Canon Law* with regard to clerics in general and deacons in particular.

Obedience and availability

8.   The rite of ordination includes a promise of obedience to the bishops: "Do you promise respect and obedience to me and to my successors?".[11] In making this promise to his bishop the deacon takes Christ, obedient par excellence (cf. *Phil* 2: 5-11), as his model. He shall conform his own obedience in listening (*Hb* 10, 5ff; *John* 4:34) and in radical availability (cf. *Lk* 9:54ff and 10:1ff) to the obedience of Christ. He shall therefore dedicate himself to working in complete conformity with the will of the Father and devote himself to the Church by means of complete availability.[12] In a spirit of prayer, with which he

---

[11] *Pontificale Romanum, De Ordinatione Episcopi, Presbyterorum et Diaconorum,* n. 201, (editio typica altera), Typis Polyglottis Vaticanis, 1990, p. 110; cf. *CIC,* canon 273.

[12] "Those dominated by an outlook of contestation or of opposition to authority cannot adequately fulfil the functions of the diaconate. The diaconate can only be conferred on those who believe in the

should be permeated, the deacon, following the example of the Lord who gave himself "unto death, death on a cross" (*Phil* 2:8), should deepen every day his total gift of self. This vision of obedience also predisposes acceptance of a more concrete detailing of the obligation assumed by the deacon at ordination, in accordance with the provisions of law: "Unless excused by a lawful impediment, clerics are obliged to accept and faithfully fulfil the office committed to them by their Ordinary".[13] This obligation is based on participation in the bishop's ministry conferred by the Sacrament of Holy Orders and by canonical mission. The extent of obedience and availability is determined by the diaconal ministry itself and by all that is objectively, immediately and directly in relation to it.

The Deacon receives office by a decree of the bishop. In his decree of appointment, the bishop shall ascribe duties to the deacon which are congruent with his personal abilities, his celibate or married state, his formation, age, and with his spiritually valid aspirations. The territory in which his ministry is to be exercised or those to whom he is to minister should be clearly specified. The decree must also indicate whether the office conferred is to be discharged on a partial or full-time basis and the priest who has the "cura animarum" where the deacon's ministry is exercised, must be named.

value of the pastoral mission of bishops and priests and in the assistance of the Holy Spirit who helps them in their activities and in the decisions they take. It should be recalled that the deacon must 'profess respect and obedience to the bishop'. The service of the deacon is directed to a particular Christian community for which he should develop a profound attachment both to its mission and divine institution" (Catechesis of JOHN PAUL II at the General Audience of 20 October 1993, n. 2, *Insegnamenti*, XVI, 2, [1993], p. 1055).

[13] *CIC*, canon 274, § 2.

Lifestyle   9.   Clerics are obliged to live in the bond of fraternity and of prayer, collaborate with each other and with the bishop to recognise and foster the mission of the faithful in the Church and in the world [14] and live in a simple, sober manner which is open to fraternal giving and sharing. [15]

Clerical garb   10.   Unlike deacons to be ordained to the priesthood, [16] who are bound by the same norms as priests in the matter, [17] permanent deacons are not obliged to wear clerical garb. Deacons who are members of institutes of consecrated life or societies of apostolic life shall adhere to the norms prescribed for them by the *Code of Canon Law*. [18]

Right   11.   In its canonical discipline, the Church recognises
of association   the right of deacons to form associations among themselves to promote their spiritual life, to carry out charitable and pious works and pursue other objectives which are consonant with their sacramental consecration and mission. [19] As with other clerics, deacons are not permitted to found, participate in or be

---

[14] "Among the duties of the deacon there is that of 'promoting and sustaining the apostolic activities of the laity'. Being more present and active in the secular world than priests, deacons should strive to promote greater closeness between ordained ministers and activities of the laity for the common service of the Kingdom of God" (Catechesis of JOHN PAUL II at the General Audience of 13 October 1993, n. 5, *Insegnamenti*, XVI, 2 [1993], pp. 1002-1003); cf. *CIC*, canon 275.

[15] Cf. *CIC*, canon 282.

[16] Cf. *CIC*, canon 288 referring to canon 284.

[17] Cf. *CIC*, canon 284; *Directory for the Ministry and Life of Priests* of the CONGREGATION FOR THE CLERGY (31 January 1994), pp. 66-67. Clarification of the PONTIFICAL COUNCIL FOR THE INTERPRETATION OF LEGISLATIVE TEXTS on the binding character of article 66 (22 October 1994) in *Sacrum Ministerium*, 2 (1995), p. 263.

[18] Cf *CIC*, canon 669.

[19] Cf. *CIC*, canon 278, §§ 1-2, explicating canon 215.

members of any association or group, even of a civil nature, which is incompatible with the clerical state or which impedes the diligent execution of their ministerial duties. They shall also avoid all associations whose nature, objectives and methods are insidious to the full hierarchical communion of the Church. Likewise, associations which are injurious to the identity of the diaconate and to the discharge of its duties for the Church's service, as well as those groups or associations which plot against the Church, are to be avoided.[20]

Associations too which, under the guise of representation, organize deacons into a form of *trade(s) unions or pressure groups,* thus reducing the sacred ministry to a secular profession or trade, are completely irreconcilable with the clerical state. The same is true of any form of association which would prejudice the direct and immediate relationship between every deacon and his bishop.

All such associations are forbidden because they are injurious to the exercise of the sacred ministry, which, in this context, is considered as no more than a subordinate activity, and because they promote conflict with the bishops who are similarly regarded purely as employers.[21]

It should be recalled that no private association may be considered an ecclesial association unless it shall have obtained prior *recognitio* of its statutes by the competent ecclesiastical authority.[22] Such au-

---

[20] Cf. *CIC*, canon 278, § 3 and canon 1374; also the declaration of the GERMAN BISHOPS' Conference "The Church and Freemasonry" (28 February 1980).

[21] CONGREGATION FOR THE CLERGY, *Quidam Episcopi* (8 March 1982), IV: AAS 74 (1982), pp. 642-645.

[22] Cf. *CIC*, canon 299, § 3, and canon 304.

thority has the right and duty to be vigilant concerning associations and the fulfilment of their statutory ends.[23]

Deacons who come from ecclesial associations or movements may continue to enjoy the spiritual benefits of such communities and may continue to draw help and support from them in their service of a particular Church.

Professional responsibilities

12. The professional activity of deacons assumes a significance which distinguishes it from that of the lay faithful.[24] Thus the secular work of permanent deacons is in some sense linked with their ministry. They should be mindful that the lay members of the faithful, in virtue of their own specific mission, are "particularly called to make the Church present and fruitful in those places and circumstances where it is only through them that she can become the salt of the earth".[25]

Derogating from what is prescribed for other clerics,[26] the present discipline of the Church does not prohibit to permanent deacons professions which involve the exercise of civil authority or the administration of temporal goods or accountable secular offices. Particular law, however, may determine otherwise, should such derogation prove inopportune.

[23] Cf *CIC*, canon 305.

[24] Cf. Allocution of JOHN PAUL II to the Bishops of Zaïre on "Ad Limina" visit, 30 April 1983, *Insegnamenti*, VI, 1 (1983), pp. 112-113. Allocution to Permanent Deacons (16 March 1985), *Insegnamenti*, VIII, 1 (1985), pp. 648-650. Cf. also idem. Allocution at the ordination of eight new Bishops in Kinshasa (4 May 1980), 3-5 *Insegnamenti*, 1 (1980), pp. 1111-1114; Catechesis at the General Audience of 6 October 1983 *Insegnamenti*, XVI, 2 (1983), pp. 951-955.

[25] *Lumen Gentium*, 33; cf. *CIC*, canon 225.

[26] Cf. *CIC*, canon 288, referring to canon 285, §§ 3-4.

In those commercial and business activities [27] permitted under particular law, deacons should exhibit honesty and ethical rectitude. They should be careful to fulfil their obligations to civil law where it is not contrary to the natural law, to the Magisterium or to the canons of the Church and to her freedom.[28]

The aforementioned derogation is not applicable to permanent deacons who are incardinated into institutes of consecrated life or societies of apostolic life.[29]

Permanent deacons must make prudent judgements and they should seek the advice of their bishops in more complex instances. Some professions, while of undoubted benefit to the community, can, when exercised by a permanent deacon, in certain circumstances, become incompatible with the pastoral responsibilities of his ministry. The competent authority, bearing in mind the requirements of ecclesial communion and of the fruitfulness of pastoral ministry, shall evaluate individual cases as they arise, including a change of profession after ordination to the permanent Diaconate.

Where there is conflict of conscience, deacons must act in conformity with the doctrine and discipline of the Church, even if this should require of them great sacrifices.

13. As sacred ministers, deacons are required to give complete priority to their ministry and to pastoral charity and "do their utmost to foster among people peace and harmony based on justice".[30] Active involvement in political parties or trades unions, in accordance with the dispositions of the Episcopal

Socio-political involvement

---

[27] Cf. *CIC*, canon 288 referring to canon 286.
[28] Cf. *CIC*, canon 222, § 2, and also canon 225, § 2.
[29] Cf. *CIC*, canon 672.
[30] Cf. *CIC*, canon 287, § 1.

Conference,[31] may be permitted in particular circumstances "for the defence of the rights of the Church or to promote the common good".[32] Deacons are strictly prohibited from all involvement with political parties or trade(s) union movements which are founded on ideologies, policies or associations incompatible with Church doctrine.

Residence   14.   Should a deacon wish to absent himself from his diocese for "a considerable period of time", he should normally obtain the permission of his Ordinary or Major Superior in accordance with the provisions of particular law.[33]

Upkeep and Insurance

Remuneration   15.   Deacons who are professionally employed are
and benefits   required to provide for their own upkeep from the ensuing emoluments.[34]

It is entirely legitimate that those who devote themselves fully to the service of God in the discharge of ecclesiastical office,[35] be equitably remunerated, since "the labourer is deserving of his wage"(*Lk* 10:7) and the Lord has disposed that those who proclaim the Gospel should live by the Gospel (cf. *1 Cor* 9:14). This does not however exclude the possibility that a cleric might wish to renounce this right, as the Apostle himself did (*1 Cor* 9:12), and otherwise make provision for himself.

It is not easy to draw up general norms concerning the upkeep of deacons which are binding in all

---

[31] Cf. *CIC*, canon 288.
[32] Cf. *CIC*, canon 287, § 2.
[33] Cf. *CIC*, canon 283.
[34] Cf. PAUL VI, Apostolic Letter *Sacrum Diaconatus Ordinem*, 21: *l.c.*, 701.
[35] Cf. *CIC*, canon 281.

circumstances, given the great diversity of situations in which deacons work, in various particular Churches and countries. In this matter, due attention must also be given to possible stipulations made in agreements between the Holy See or Episcopal Conferences and governments. In such circumstances, particular law should determine appropriately in the matter.

16. Since clerics dedicate themselves in an active and concrete way to the ecclesiastical ministry, they have a right to sustenance which includes "a remuneration that befits their condition" [36] and to social security. [37]

With regard to married deacons the *Code of Canon Law* provides that: "married deacons who dedicate themselves full-time to the ecclesiastical ministry deserve remuneration sufficient to provide for themselves and their families. Those, however, who receive remuneration by reason of a secular profession which they exercise or have exercised are to see to their own and to their families' needs from that income". [38] In prescribing "adequate" remuneration, parameters of evaluation are also: personal condition, the nature of the office exercised, circumstances of time and place, material needs of the minister (including those

[36] "Since clerics dedicate themselves to the ecclesiastical ministry, they deserve the remuneration that befits their condition, taking into account the nature of their office and the conditions of time and place. It is to be such that it provides for the necessities of their life and for the just remuneration of those whose services they need" (*CIC,* canon 281, § 1).

[37] "Suitable provision is likewise to be made for such social welfare as they may need in infirmity, sickness or old age" (*CIC,* canon 281, § 2).

[38] *CIC,* canon 281, § 3. The canonical term "remuneration" as distinct from civil law usage, denotes more than a stipend in the technical sense of this term. It connotes that income, due in justice, which permits a decent upkeep, congruent with the ministry.

of the families of married deacons), just recompense of those in his service — the same general criteria, in fact, which apply to all clerics.

In order to provide for the sustenance of clerics ministering in dioceses, every particular Church is obliged to constitute a special fund which "collects offerings and temporal goods for the support of the clergy".[39]

Social security for clerics is to be provided by another fund, unless other provision has been made.[40]

Celibate deacons without other remuneration

17. Celibate deacons who minister full-time in a diocese, have a right to be remunerated according to the general principle of law [41] should they have no other source of income.

Married deacons without other remuneration

18. Married deacons who minister full-time and who do not receive income from any other source are to be remunerated, in accordance with the aforementioned general principle, so that they may be able to provide for themselves and for their families.[42]

Married deacons with income

19. Married deacons who minister full-time or part-time and who receive income from a secular profession which they exercise or have exercised are obliged to provide for themselves and for their families from such income.[43]

Reimbursement of expenses

20. It is for particular law to provide opportune norms in the complex matter of reimbursing expenses, including, for example, that those entities and parishes which benefit from the ministry of a deacon have an obligation to reimburse him those expenses incurred in the exercise of his ministry.

[39] *Ibid.*, canon 1274, § 1.
[40] *Ibid.*, canon 1274, § 2.
[41] *Ibid.*, canon 281, § 1.
[42] Cf. *ibidem,* canon 281, § 3.
[43] Cf. *ibid.*, canon 281, § 3.

Particular law may also determine the obligations devolving on the diocese when a deacon, through no fault of his own, becomes unemployed. Likewise, it will be opportune to define the extent of diocesan liability with regard to the widows and orphans of deceased deacons. Where possible, deacons, before ordination, should subscribe to a mutual assurance (insurance) policy which affords cover for these eventualities.

Loss of the diaconal state

21.   Trusting to the perennial fidelity of God, the deacon is called to live his Order with generous dedication and ever renewed perseverance. Sacred ordination, once validly received, can never be rendered null. Nevertheless, loss of the clerical state may occur in conformity with the canonical norms.[44]

---

[44] Cf. *ibid.*, canons 290-293.

2

THE DIACONAL MINISTRY

Diaconal functions

Threefold   22.   The Second Vatican Council synthesized the
diaconia   ministry of deacons in the threefold "diaconia of the
liturgy, the word and of charity".[45] In this way diaconal participation through the ordained ministry in
the one and triple *munus* of Christ is expressed. The
deacon "is *teacher* in so far as he preaches and bears
witness to the word of God; he *sanctifies* when he
administers the Sacrament of Baptism, the Holy Eucharist and the sacramentals, he participates at the
celebration of Holy Mass as a "minister of the
Blood", and conserves and distributes the Blessed Eucharist; he is a *guide* in as much as he animates the
community or a section of ecclesial life.[46] Thus deacons assist and serve the bishops and priests who
preside at every liturgy, are watchful of doctrine and
guide the people of God.

The ministry of deacons, in the service of the
community of the faithful, should "collaborate in

---

[45] SECOND VATICAN COUNCIL, Dogmatic Constitution *Lumen Gentium*, 29.

[46] JOHN PAUL II, Allocution to permanent deacons (16 March
1985), n. 2: *Insegnamenti*, VIII, 1 (1985), p. 649; cf. SECOND
VATICAN COUNCIL, Dogmatic Constitution. *Lumen Gentium*, 29;
CIC, canon 1008.

building up the unity of Christians without prejudice and without inopportune initiatives".[47] It should cultivate those "human qualities which make a person acceptable to others, credible, vigilant about his language and his capacity to dialogue, so as to acquire a truly ecumenical attitude".[48]

Diaconia of the word

23. The bishop, during the rite of ordination, gives the book of the Gospels to the deacon saying: "Receive the Gospel of Christ whose herald you have become".[49] Like priests, deacons are commended to all by their conduct, their preaching of the mystery of Christ, by transmitting Christian doctrine and by devoting attention to the problems of our time. The principal function of the deacon, therefore, is to collaborate with the bishop and the priests in the exercise of a ministry [50] which is not of their own wisdom but of the word of God, calling all to conversion and holiness.[51] He prepares for such a ministry by careful study of Sacred

Proclaiming the Gospel

[47] Pontifical Council for the Promotion of Christian Unity *Directory on the applications of the principles and norms on ecumenism*, (25 March 1993), 71: *AAS* 85 (1993), p. 1069; cf. Congregation for the Doctrine of the Faith, *Communionis notio* (28 May 1992), *AAS* 85 [1993], pp. 838f.

[48] *Ibid.*, 70: *l.c.*, p. 1068.

[49] *Pontificale Romanum*, n. 210: ed. cit., p. 125: "Accipe Evangelium Christi, cuius praeco effectus es; et vide, ut quod legeris credas, quod credideris doceas, quod docueris imiteris".

[50] Cf. Second Vatican Council, Dogmatic Constitution *Lumen Gentium*, 29. "Deacons are also to serve the People of God in the ministry of the word, in union with the bishop and his *presbyterium*" (*CIC*, canon 757); "By their preaching, deacons participate in the priestly ministry" (John Paul II, Allocution to Priests, Deacons, Religious and Seminarians in the Basilica of the Oratory of St. Joseph, Montreal, Canada (11 September 1984), n. 9: *Insegnamenti*, VII, 2 (1984), p. 436.

[51] Cf. Second Vatican Council, Decree *Presbyterorum Ordinis*, 4.

Scripture, of Tradition, of the liturgy and of the life of the Church.[52] Moreover, in interpreting and applying the sacred deposit, the deacon is obliged to be directed by the Magisterium of those who are "witnesses of divine and Catholic truth",[53] the Roman Pontiff and the bishops in communion with him,[54] so as to teach and propose the mystery of Christ fully and faithfully.[55]

It is also necessary that he learn the art of communicating the faith effectively and integrally to contemporary man, in diverse cultural circumstances and stages of life.[56]

Minister of the Word

24. It is for the deacon to proclaim the Gospel and preach the word of God.[57] Deacons have the faculty to preach everywhere, in accordance with the conditions established by law.[58] This faculty is founded on the Sacrament of Ordination and should be exercised with at least the tacit consent of the rector of the churches concerned and with that humility proper to one who is servant and not master of the word of God. In this respect the warning of the Apostle is always relevant: "Since we have this ministry through the mercy shown to us, we are not discouraged. Rather we have renounced shameful, hidden things; not acting deceitfully or falsifying the word of God, but by the open declara-

---

[52] Cf. SECOND VATICAN COUNCIL, Dogmatic Constitution *Dei Verbum*, 25; CONGREGATION FOR CATHOLIC EDUCATION, circular letter *Come è a conoscenza*; *CIC*, canon 760.

[53] SECOND VATICAN COUNCIL, Dogmatic Constitution *Lumen Gentium*, 25a; Dogmatic Constitution *Dei Verbum*, 10a.

[54] Cf. *CIC*, canon 753.

[55] Cf. *ibid.*, canon 760.

[56] Cf. *ibid.*, canon 769.

[57] Cf. *Institutio Generalis Missalis Romani*, n. 61: *Missale Romanum*, Ordo lectionis Missae, *Praenotanda*, n. 8, 24 and 50: ed. typica altera, 1981.

[58] Cf. *CIC*, canon 764.

90

tion of the truth we commend ourselves to everybody's conscience in the sight God" (2 Cor 4: 1-2).[59]

25.   When the deacon presides at a liturgical celebration, in accordance with the relevant norms,[60] he shall give due importance to the homily, since it "proclaims the marvels worked by God in the mystery of Christ, present and effective in the liturgical celebrations".[61] Deacons should be trained carefully to prepare their homilies in prayer, in study of the sacred texts, in perfect harmony with the Magisterium and in keeping with the situation of those to whom they preach.

Homily and catechesis

In order to assist the Christian faithful to grow in knowledge of their faith in Christ, to strengthen it by reception of the sacraments and to express it in their family, professional and social lives,[62] much attention must be given to catechesis of the faithful of all stages of Christian living. With growing secularization and the ever greater challenges posed for man and for the Gospel by contemporary society, the need for complete, faithful and lucid catechesis becomes all the more pressing.

---

[59] CONGREGATION FOR THE CLERGY, Directory on the Ministry and Life of Priests, *Tota Ecclesia* (31 January 1994), nn. 45-47: *l.c.,* 43-48.

[60] Cf. *Institutio Generalis Missalis Romani,* nn. 42, 61; CONGREGATION FOR THE CLERGY, PONTIFICAL COUNCIL FOR THE LAITY, CONGREGATION FOR THE DOCTRINE OF THE FAITH, CONGREGATION FOR DIVINE WORSHIP AND THE DISCIPLINE OF THE SACRAMENTS, CONGREGATION FOR BISHOPS, CONGREGATION FOR THE EVANGELIZATION OF PEOPLES, CONGREGATION FOR THE INSTITUTES OF CONSECRATED LIFE AND THE SOCIETIES OF APOSTOLIC LIFE, PONTIFICAL COUNCIL FOR THE INTERPRETATION OF LEGISLATIVE TEXTS, Instruction concerning some questions on the collaboration of the lay faithful in the ministry of priests, *Ecclesiae de Mysterio* (15 August 1997), art. 3.

[61] SECOND VATICAN COUNCIL, Constitution *Sacrosanctum Concilium,* 35; cf. 52; *CIC,* canon 767, § 1.

[62] Cf. *CIC,* canon 779; cf. CONGREGATION FOR THE CLERGY, *General Directory for Catechesis,* (15 agosto 1997) n. 216.

26. Contemporary society requires a new evangelization which demands a greater and more generous effort on the part of ordained ministers. Deacons, "nourished by prayer and above all by love of the Eucharist",[63] in addition to their involvement in diocesan and parochial programmes of catechesis, of evangelization and of preparation for the reception of the Sacraments, should strive to transmit the word in their professional lives, either explicitly or merely by their active presence in places where public opinion is formed and ethical norms are applied — such as the social services or organisations promoting the rights of the family or life. They should also be aware of the great possibilities for the ministry of the word in the area of religious and moral instruction in schools,[64] in Catholic and civil universities [65] and by adequate use of modern means of social communication.[66]

In addition to indispensable orthodoxy of doctrine, these *new fields demand* specialized training, but they are very effective means of bringing the Gospel to contemporary man and society.[67]

Finally, deacons are reminded that they are obliged to submit, before its publication, written material concerning faith or morals,[68] to the judgement of their Ordinaries. It is also necessary to obtain the permission of the Ordinary before writing in publications which habitually attack the Catholic religion or good morals. They are also bound to adhere to the norms established by

---

[63] PAUL VI, Apostolic Exhortation, *Evangelii Nuntiandi*, 8 December 1975): *AAS* 68 (1976), pp. 576.
[64] Cf. *ibid.,* canons 804-805.
[65] Cf. *ibid.,* canon 810.
[66] Cf. *ibid.,* canon 761.
[67] Cf. *ibid.,* canon 822.
[68] Cf. *ibid.,* canon 823, § 1.

the Episcopal Conference [69] when involved in radio or television broadcasts.

In every case, the deacon should hold before him the primary and indefeasible necessity of always presenting the truth without compromise.

27. The deacon will be aware that the Church is missionary [70] by her very nature, both because her origin is in the missions of the Son and the Holy Spirit, according to the eternal plan of the Father and because she has received an explicit mandate from the risen Lord to preach the Gospel to all creation and to baptize those who believe (cf. *Mk* 16, 15-16; *Mt* 28:19). Deacons are ministers of the Church and thus, although incardinated into a particular Church, they are not exempt from the missionary obligation of the universal Church. Hence they should always remain open to the *missio ad gentes* to the extent that their professional or — if married — family obligations permit. [71] *Missionary endeavour*

The deacon's ministry of service is linked with the missionary dimension of the Church: the missionary efforts of the deacon will embrace the ministry of the word, the liturgy, and works of charity which, in their turn, are carried into daily life. Mission includes witness to Christ in a secular profession or occupation.

Diaconia of the liturgy

28. The rite of ordination emphasizes another aspect of the diaconal ministry — ministry at the altar. [72] *Serving the work of sanctification*

Deacons receive the Sacrament of Orders, so as to serve as a vested minister in the sanctification of

---

[69] *Ibid.,* canon 831, §§ 1-2.
[70] SECOND VATICAN COUNCIL, Decree *Ad Gentes*, 2a.
[71] Cf. *CIC,* canons 784, 786.
[72] SECOND VATICAN COUNCIL, Decree *Ad Gentes*, 16; *Pontificale Romanum*, n. 207: ed. cit., p. 122 (*Prex Ordinationis*).

the Christian community, in hierarchical communion with the bishop and priests. They provide a sacramental assistance to the ministry of the bishop and, subordinately, to that of the priests which is intrinsic, fundamental and distinct.

Clearly, this diaconia at the altar, since founded on the Sacrament of Orders, differs in essence from any liturgical ministry entrusted to the lay faithful. The liturgical ministry of the deacon is also distinct from that of the ordained priestly ministry.[73]

Thus, in the Eucharistic Sacrifice, the deacon does not celebrate the mystery: rather, he effectively represents on the one hand, the people of God and, specifically, helps them to unite their lives to the offering of Christ; while on the other, in the name of Christ himself, he helps the Church to participate in the fruits of that sacrifice.

Since "the liturgy is the summit towards which the activity of the Church is directed and the font from which all her power flows",[74] this prerogative of diaconal ordination is also the font of sacramental grace which nourishes the entire ministry. Careful and profound theological and liturgical preparation must precede reception of that grace to enable the deacon to participate worthily in the celebration of the sacraments and sacramentals.

Style of celebrating

29.   While exercising his ministry, the deacon should maintain a lively awareness that "every liturgical celebration, because it is an action of Christ the Priest and of his Body which is the Church, is a sacred action surpassing all others. No other action of the

---

[73] Cf. Second Vatican Council, Dogmatic Constitution *Lumen Gentium*, 29.

[74] Second Vatican Council, Constitution *Sacrosanctum Concilium*, 10.

Church can equal its efficacy by the same title and to the same degree".[75] The liturgy is the source of grace and sanctification. Its efficacy derives from Christ the Redeemer and does not depend on the holiness of the minister. This certainty should cause the deacon to grow in humility since he can never compromise the salvific work of Christ. At the same time it should inspire him to holiness of life so that he may be a worthy minister of the liturgy. Liturgical actions cannot be reduced to mere private or social actions which can be celebrated by anybody since they belong to the Body of the universal Church.[76] Deacons shall observe devoutly the liturgical norms proper to the sacred mysteries so as to bring the faithful to a conscious participation in the liturgy, to fortify their faith, give worship to God and sanctify the Church.[77]

30. According to the tradition of the Church and the provisions of law,[78] deacons "assist the bishop and priests in the celebration of the divine mysteries".[79] They should therefore work to promote liturgical celebrations which involve the whole assembly, fostering the interior participation of the faithful in the liturgy and the exercise of the various ministries.[80]

Assistance to bishops and priests at liturgical celebrations

They should be mindful of the importance of the aesthetical dimension which conveys to the whole person the beauty of what is being celebrated. Music and song, even in its simplest form, the preached

---

[75] *Ibid.,* 7d.

[76] Cf. *ibid.,* 22, 3; *CIC,* canons 841, 846.

[77] Cf. *CIC,* canon 840.

[78] *Catechism of the Catholic Church,* n. 1570; cf. *Caeremoniale Episcoporum,* nn. 23-26.

[79] "Deacons have a share in the celebration of divine worship in accordance with the provisions of law" (*CIC,* canon 835, § 3).

[80] Cf. SECOND VATICAN COUNCIL, Constitution *Sacrosanctum Concilium,* 26-27.

word and the communion of the faithful who live the peace and forgiveness of Christ, form a precious heritage which the deacon should foster.

The deacon is to observe faithfully the rubrics of the liturgical books without adding, omitting or changing of his own volition [81] what they require. Manipulation of the liturgy is tantamount to depriving it of the riches of the mystery of Christ, whom it contains, and may well signify presumption toward what has been established by the Church's wisdom. Deacons, therefore, should confine themselves to those things, and only to those things, in which they are properly competent.[82] For the Sacred Liturgy they should vest worthily and with dignity, in accordance with the prescribed liturgical norms.[83] The dalmatic, in its appropriate liturgical colours, together with the alb, cincture and stole, "constitutes the liturgical dress proper to deacons".[84]

The ministry of deacons also includes preparation of the faithful for reception of the sacraments and their pastoral care after having received them.

---

[81] Cf. *CIC,* canon 846, § 1.

[82] Cf. SECOND VATICAN COUNCIL, Constitutions *Sacrosanctum Concilium,* 28.

[83] Cf. *CIC,* canon 929.

[84] Cf. *Institutio generalis Missalis Romani,* nn, 81b, 300, 302; *Institutio generalis Liturgiae Horarum,* n. 255; *Pontificale Romanum,* nn. 23, 24, 28, 29, editio typica, Typis Polyglottis Vaticanis 1977, pp. 29 and 90; *Rituale Romanum,* n. 36, editio typica, Typis Polyglottis Vaticanis 1985, p. 18; *Ordo Coronandi Imaginem Beatae Mariae Virginis,* n. 12, editio typica, Typis Polyglottis Vaticanis 1981, p. 10; CONGREGATION FOR DIVINE WORSHIP, Directory for celebrations in the absence of a priest, *Christi Ecclesia,* n 38, in "Notitiae" 24 (1988), pp. 388-389; *Pontificale Romanum,* nn. 188: ("Immediate post Precem Ordinationis, Ordinati stola diaconali et dalmatica induuntur quo eorum ministerium abhinc in liturgia peragendum manifestatur") and 190; ed. cit., pp. 102, 103; *Caeremoniale Episcoporum,* n. 67, editio typica, Libreria Editrice Vaticana 1995, pp. 28-29.

31. The deacon, together with the bishop and *Baptism* priest, is the ordinary minister of Baptism.[85] The exercise of this power requires either the permission of the parish priest, since he enjoys the particular right of baptizing those entrusted to his pastoral care,[86] or the presence of necessity.[87] In preparing for the reception of this sacrament, the ministry of the deacon is especially important.

32. At the celebration of the Holy Eucharist, the *Holy Eucharist* deacon assists those who preside at the assembly and consecrate the Body and Blood of the Lord — that is the bishop and his priests [88] — according to the norms established by the *Institutio Generalis* of the Roman Missal,[89] and thus manifests Christ, the Servant. He is close to the priest during the celebration of the Mass [90] and helps him, especially if the priest is blind, infirm or feeble. At the altar he serves the chalice and the book. He proposes the intentions of the bidding prayers to the faithful and invites them to exchange the sign of peace. In the absence of other ministers, he discharges, when necessary, their office too.

The deacon may not pronounce the words of the eucharistic prayer, nor those of the collects nor may he use the gestures which are proper to those who consecrate the Body and Blood of the Lord.[91]

---

[85] *CIC*, canon 861, § 1.

[86] Cf. *ibid.*, canon 530, n. 1°.

[87] Cf. *ibid.*, canon 862.

[88] Cf. PAUL VI, Apostolic Letter *Sacrum Diaconatus Ordinem*, V, 22, 1: *l.c.*, 701.

[89] Cf. *Institutio Generalis Missalis Romani*, nn. 61; 127-141.

[90] Cf. *CIC*, canon 930, § 2.

[91] Cf. *ibid.*, canon 907; CONGREGATION FOR THE CLERGY etc., Instruction *Ecclesiae de Mysterio* (15 August 1997), art. 6.

The deacon properly proclaims from the books of Sacred Scripture.[92]

As an ordinary minister of Holy Communion,[93] the deacon distributes the Body of Christ to the faithful during the celebration of the Mass and, outside of it, administers Viaticum [94] to the sick. He is equally an ordinary minister of exposition of the Most Blessed Sacrament and of eucharistic benediction.[95] It falls to the deacon to preside at Sunday celebrations in the absence of a priest.[96]

Marriage 33. The pastoral care of families, for which the bishop is primarily responsible, may be entrusted to deacons. In supporting families in their difficulties and sufferings,[97] this responsibility will extend from moral and liturgical questions to difficulties of a social and personal nature, and can be exercised at diocesan or, subject to the authority of the parish priest, local level in promoting the catechesis of Christian marriage, the personal preparation of future spouses, the fruitful celebration of marriage and help offered to couples after marriage.[98]

Married deacons can be of much assistance in promoting the Gospel value of conjugal love, the virtues which protect it and the practice of parent-

---

[92] Cf. PAUL VI, Apostolic Letter *Sacrum Diaconatus Ordinem*, V, 22, 6: *l.c.,* 702.

[93] Cf. *CIC,* canon 910, § 1.

[94] Cf. *ibid.,* canon 911, § 2.

[95] Cf. *ibid.,* canon 943 and also Pope PAUL VI, Apostolic Letter *Sacrum Diaconatus Ordinem*, V, 22, 3: *l.c.,* 702.

[96] Cf. CONGREGATION FOR DIVINE WORSHIP, Directory for celebrations in the absence of a priest, *Christi Ecclesia,* n. 38: *l.c.,* 388-389; CONGREGATION FOR THE CLERGY etc., Instruction *Ecclesiae de Mysterio* (15 August 1997), art. 7.

[97] Cf. JOHN PAUL II, Post-Synodal Apostolic Exhortation *Familiaris Consortio,* 73: AAS 74 (22 November, 1982), pp. 107-171.

[98] Cf. *CIC,* canon 1063.

hood which can truly be regarded as responsible, from a human and Christian point of view.

Where deacons have been duly delegated by the parish priest or the local Ordinary, they may assist at the celebration of marriages *extra Missam* and pronounce the nuptial blessing in the name of the Church.[99] They may also be given general delegation, in accordance with the prescribed conditions,[100] which may only be subdelegated, however, in the manner specified by the *Code of Canon Law*.[101]

34. It is defined doctrine,[102] that the administration of the Sacrament of the Anointing of the Sick is reserved to bishops and priests since this sacrament involves the forgiveness of sins and the worthy reception of the Holy Eucharist, but, the pastoral care of the sick may be entrusted to deacons. Active service to alleviate the suffering of the sick, catechesis in preparation for the reception of the Sacrament of Anointing of the Sick, preparing the faithful for death in the absence of a priest, and the administration of Viaticum according to the prescribed rites, are means by which deacons may bring the love of the Church to the suffering faithful.[103]

Pastoral care of the Sick

---

[99] Cf. SECOND VATICAN COUNCIL, Constitution *Lumen Gentium* 29; *CIC*, canon 1108, §§ 1-2; *Ordo Celebrandi Matrimonii*, ed. typica altera 1991, 24.

[100] Cf. *CIC*, canon 1111, §§ 1-2.

[101] Cf. *ibidem*, canon 137, §§ 3-4.

[102] *Exultate Deo* of the COUNCIL OF FLORENCE (DS 1325); *Doctrina de sacramento extremae unctionis* of the COUNCIL OF TRENT, cap. 3 (DS 1697) and cap. 4 *de extrema unctione* (DS 1719).

[103] Cf. PAUL VI, Apostolic Letter *Sacrum Diaconatus Ordinem* II, 10: *l.c.*,699; CONGREGATION FOR THE CLERGY etc., Instruction, *Ecclesiae de Mysterio* (15 August 1997), art. 9.

35. Deacons have an obligation, established by the Church, to celebrate the Liturgy of the Hours with which the entire Mystical Body is united to the prayer Christ the Head offers to the Father. Mindful of this obligation, they shall celebrate the Liturgy of the Hours every day according to the approved liturgical books and in the manner determined by the respective Episcopal Conference.[104] Furthermore, they should strive to promote participation by the greater Christian community in this Liturgy, which is never private, but an action proper to the entire Church,[105] even when celebrated individually.

36. The deacon is the minister of sacramentals, that is of "sacred signs which bear a resemblance to the sacraments (and) signify effects, particularly of a spiritual nature, which are obtained through the Church's intercession".[106]

The deacon may therefore impart those blessings most closely linked to ecclesial and sacramental life which are expressly permitted to him by law.[107] It is for the deacon to conduct exequies celebrated outside of Holy Mass, as well as the rite of Christian burial.[108]

When a priest is present or available, however, such tasks must be given to him.[109]

---

[104] Cf. *CIC,* canon 276, § 2, n. 3°.

[105] Cf. *Institutio Generalis Liturgiae Horarum,* nn. 20; 255-256.

[106] Cf. SECOND VATICAN COUNCIL, Constitution *Sacrosanctum Concilium* 60; *CIC,* canon 1166 and canon 1168; *Catechism of the Catholic Church,* n. 1667.

[107] Cf. *CIC,* canon 1169, § 3.

[108] Cf. PAUL VI, Apostolic Letter *Sacrum Diaconatus Ordinem* V, 22, 5: *l.c.,* 702; also *Ordo Exsequiarum,* 19; CONGREGATION FOR THE CLERGY etc., Instruction *Ecclesiae de Mysterio* (15 August 1997), art. 12.

[109] Cf. *Rituale Romanum - De Benedictionibus,* n. 18 c.: ed. cit, p. 14.

The Diaconia of Charity

37. In virtue of the Sacrament of Orders, deacons, in communion with the bishop and the diocesan presbyterate, participate in the same pastoral functions,[110] but exercise them differently in serving and assisting the bishop and his priests. Since this participation is brought about by the sacrament, they serve God's people in the name of Christ. For this reason, they exercise it in humility and charity, and, according to the words of St Polycarp, they must always be "merciful, zealous and let them walk according to the truth of the Lord who became servant of all".[111] Their authority, therefore, exercised in hierarchical communion with the bishop and his priests, and required by the same unity of consecration and mission,[112] is a service of charity which seeks to help and foster all members of a particular Church, so that they may participate, in a spirit of communion and according to their proper charisms, in the life and mission of the Church.

Servants of God's People

38. In the ministry of charity, deacons should conform themselves in the likeness of Christ the Servant, whom they represent and, above all, they should be "dedicated to works of charity and to administration".[113] Thus, in the prayer of ordination, the bishop implores God the Father that they may be "full of all the virtues, sincere in charity, solicitous towards the weak and the poor, humble in their service... may they be the image of your Son who did not come to

The Service of Charity

---

[110] Cf. *CIC*, canon 129, § 1.
[111] St. Polycarp, *Epist. ad Philippenses*, 5, 2; F. X. Funk (ed.), I, p. 300; cited in *Lumen Gentium*, 29.
[112] Cf. Paul VI, Apostolic Letter *Sacrum Diaconatus Ordinem l.c.*, 698.
[113] Second Vatican Council, Dogmatic Constitution *Lumen Gentium*, 29.

be served but to serve".[114] By word and example they should work so that all the faithful, in imitation of Christ, may place themselves at the constant service of their brothers and sisters.

Diocesan and parochial works of charity, which are among the primary duties of bishops and priests are entrusted by them, as attested by Tradition, to servants in the ecclesiastical ministry, that is, to deacons.[115] So too is the service of charity in Christian education; in training preachers, youth groups, and lay groups; in promoting life in all its phases and transforming the world according to the Christian order.[116] In all of these areas the ministry of deacons is particularly valuable, since today the spiritual and material needs of man, to which the Church is called to respond, are greatly diversified. They should, therefore, strive to serve all the faithful without discrimination, while devoting particular care to the suffering and the sinful. As ministers of Christ and of his Church, they must be able to transcend all ideologies and narrow party interests, lest they deprive the Church's mission of its strength which is the love of Christ. Diaconia should bring man to an experience of God's love and move him to conversion by opening his heart to the work of grace.

[114] *Pontificale Romanum - De ordinatione Episcopi, presbyterorum et diaconorum*, n. 207, p. 122 (Prex Ordinationis).
[115] HIPPOLYTUS, *Traditio Apostolica*, 8, 24; *S. Ch.* 11 bis pp. 58-63, 98-99; *Didascalia Apostolorum* (Syriac), chapters III and IX; A. VÖÖBUS (ed) *The "Didascalia Apostolorum" in Syriac* (original text in Syriac with an English translation), CSCO vol. I, n. 402 (tome 176), pp. 29-30; vol. II, n. 408 (tome 180), pp. 120-129; *Didascalia Apostolorum*, III (19), 1-7: F. X. FUNK (ed.), *Didascalia et Constitutiones Apostolorum*, Paderbornae 1906, I, pp. 212-216; SECOND VATICAN COUNCIL, Decree *Christus Dominus*, 13.
[116] SECOND VATICAN COUNCIL, Pastoral Constitution *Gaudium et Spes*, 40-45.

The charitable function of deacons "also involves appropriate service in the administration of goods and in the Church's charitable activities. In this regard, deacons "discharge the duties of charity and administration in the name of the hierarchy and also provide social services".[117] Hence, deacons may be appointed to the office of diocesan oeconomus [118] and likewise nominated to the diocesan finance council.[119]

The canonical mission of permanent deacons

39. The three contexts of the diaconal ministry, depending on circumstances, may absorb, to varying degrees, a large proportion of every deacon's activity. Together, however, they represent a unity in service at the level of divine Revelation: the ministry of the word leads to ministry at the altar, which in turn prompts the transformation of life by the liturgy, resulting in charity. "If we consider the deep spiritual nature of this diaconia, then we shall better appreciate the inter-relationship between the three areas of ministry traditionally associated with the diaconate, that is, the ministry of the word, the ministry of the altar and the ministry of charity. Depending on the circumstances, one or other of these may take on special importance in the individual work of a dea-

Exercise of the threefold diaconia

---

[117] PAUL VI, Apostolic Letter *Sacrum Diaconatus Ordinem*, V, 22, 9; *l.c.,* 702. Cf. JOHN PAUL II, Catechesis at the General Audience of 13 October 1993, n. 5: *Insegnamenti* XVI, 2 (1993), pp. 1000-1004.

[118] Cf. *CIC,* canon 494.

[119] Cf. *CIC,* canon 493.

con, but these three ministries are inseparably joined in God's plan for redemption".[120]

Conferring of office 40.   Throughout history the service of deacons has taken on various forms so as to satisfy the diverse needs of the Christian community and to enable that community to exercise its mission of charity. It is for the bishops alone,[121] since they rule and have charge of the particular Churches "as Vicars and legates of Christ",[122] to confer ecclesiastical office on each deacon according to the norm of law. In conferring such office, careful attention should be given to both the pastoral needs and the personal, family (in the case of married deacons), and professional situation of permanent deacons. In every case it is important, however, that deacons fully exercise their ministry, in preaching, in the liturgy and in charity to the extent that circumstances permit. They should not be relegated to marginal duties, be made merely to act as substitutes, nor discharge duties normally entrusted to non-ordained members of the faithful. Only in this way will the true identity of permanent deacons as ministers of Christ become apparent and the impression avoided that deacons are simply lay people particularly involved in the life of the Church.

For the good of the deacon and to prevent improvisation, ordination should be accompanied by a clear investiture of pastoral responsibility.

Parish Ministry 41.   While assuming different forms, the diaconal ministry, ordinarily finds proper scope for its exercise

---

[120] Cf. JOHN PAUL II, Address to the permanent deacons of the USA, Detroit (19 September 1987), n. 3, *Insegnamenti*, X, 3 (1987), p. 656.

[121] Cf. *CIC*, canon 157.

[122] SECOND VATICAN COUNCIL, Dogmatic Constitution *Lumen Gentium*, 27a.

in the various sectors of diocesan and parochial pastoral action.

The bishop may give deacons the task of co-operating with a parish priest in the parish [123] entrusted to him or in the pastoral care of several parishes entrusted *in solidum* to one or more priests.[124]

Where permanent deacons participate in the pastoral care of parishes which do not, because of a shortage, have the immediate benefit of a parish priest,[125] they always have precedence over the non-ordained faithful. In such cases, it is necessary to specify that the moderator of the parish is a priest and that he is its proper pastor. To him alone has been entrusted the *cura animarum,* in which he is assisted by the deacon.

Deacons may also be called to guide dispersed Christian communities in the name of the bishop or the parish priest.[126] "This is a missionary function to be carried out in those territories, environments, social strata and groups where priests are lacking or cannot be easily found. In particular, in those areas where no priest is available to celebrate the Eucharist, the deacon brings together and guides the community in a celebration of the word with the distribution of Holy Communion which has been duly reserved.[127] When deacons supply in places where there is a shortage of priests, they do so by ecclesial man-

---

[123] Cf. *CIC,* canon 519.
[124] Cf. *CIC,* canon 517, § 1.
[125] Cf. *CIC,* canon 517, § 2.
[126] Cf. PAUL VI, Apostolic Letter *Sacrum Diaconatus Ordinem,* V, 22, 10; *l.c.,* 702.
[127] Cf. *CIC,* canon 1248 § 2; CONGREGATION FOR DIVINE WORSHIP, Directory for celebrations in the absence of the priest, *Christi Ecclesia,* 29, *l.c.,* 386.

date".[128] At such celebrations, prayers will always be offered for an increase of vocations to the priesthood whose indispensable nature shall be clearly emphasized. Where deacons are available, participation in the pastoral care of the faithful may not be entrusted to a lay person or to a community of lay persons. Similarly where deacons are available, it is they who preside at such Sunday celebrations.

The competence of deacons should always be clearly specified in writing when they are assigned office.

Those means which encourage constructive and patient collaboration between deacons and others involved in the pastoral ministry should be promoted with generosity and conviction. While it is a duty of deacons to respect the office of parish priest and to work in communion with all who share in his pastoral care, they also have the right to be accepted and fully recognised by all. Where the bishop has deemed it opportune to institute parish pastoral councils, deacons appointed to participate in the pastoral care of such parishes are members of these councils by right.[129] Above all else, a true charity should prevail which recognises in every ministry a gift of the Spirit destined to build up the Body of Christ.

Diocesan Ministry 42. Numerous opportunities for the fruitful exercise of the ministry of deacons arise at diocesan level. Indeed, when they possess the necessary requirements, deacons may act as members of diocesan bodies, in

---

[128] JOHN PAUL II, Catechesis at the General Audience of 13 October 1993, n. 4: *Insegnamenti* XVI, 2 (1993), p. 1002.
[129] Cf. PAUL VI, Apostolic Letter *Sacrum Diaconatus Ordinem*, V, 24; *l.c.*, 702; *CIC,* canon 536.

particular diocesan pastoral councils [130] and diocesan finance councils, and take part in diocesan synods. [131]

They may not, however, act as members of the council of priests, since this body exclusively represents the presbyterate. [132]

In the diocesan curia deacons in possession of the necessary requirements, may exercise the office of chancellor, [133] judge, [134] assessor, [135] auditor, [136] promotor iustitiae, defensor vinculi [137] and notary. [138]

Deacons may not, however, be constituted judicial vicars, adjunct judicial vicars or vicars forane, since these offices are reserved for priests. [139]

Other areas in which deacons may exercise their ministry include diocesan commissions, pastoral work in specific social contexts — especially the pastoral care of the family — or among particular groups with special pastoral needs, such as ethnic minorities.

In the exercise of the above offices, the deacon should recall that every action in the Church should be informed by charity and service to all. In judicial, administrative and organizational matters, deacons should always strive to avoid unnecessary forms of

---

[130] Cf. PAUL VI, Apostolic Letter *Sacrum Diaconatus Ordinem*, V, 24; *l.c.*, 702; *CIC*, canon 512, § 1.

[131] Cf. *CIC*, canon 463, § 2.

[132] Cf. SECOND VATICAN COUNCIL, Dogmatic Constitution *Lumen Gentium*, 28; Decree *Christus Dominus*, 27; Decree *Presbyterorum Ordinis*, 7; *CIC*, canon 495, § 1.

[133] *CIC*, canon 482.

[134] *CIC*, canon 1421, § 1.

[135] *CIC*, canon 1424.

[136] *CIC*, canon 1428, § 2.

[137] *CIC*, canon 1435.

[138] *CIC*, canon 483, § 1.

[139] *CIC*, canon 1420, § 4, canon 553 § 1.

bureaucracy, lest they deprive their ministry of pastoral meaning and value. Those deacons who are called to exercise such offices should be placed so as to discharge duties which are proper to the diaconate, in order to preserve the integrity of the diaconal ministry.

3

THE SPIRITUALITY OF THE DEACON

Contemporary context

43. The Church, gathered together by Christ and guided by the Holy Spirit according to the providence of God the Father, lives and proclaims the Gospel in concrete historical circumstances. While present in the world, she is nonetheless a pilgrim [140] on the way to the fullness of the Kingdom.[141] "The world which she has in mind is the whole human family seen in the context of everything which envelopes it: it is the world as the theatre of human history, bearing the marks of its travail, its triumphs and failures, the world, which in the Christian vision has been created and is sustained by its Maker, which has been freed from the slavery of sin by Christ, who was crucified and rose again in order to break the stranglehold of the evil one, so that it might be fashioned anew according to God's design and brought to its fulfilment".[142]

The Church in the world

The deacon, as a member and minister of the Church, should be mindful of this reality in his life and ministry. He should be conversant with contem-

[140] SECOND VATICAN COUNCIL, Constitution *Sacrosanctum Concilium*, 2.
[141] SECOND VATICAN COUNCIL, Dogmatic Constitution *Lumen Gentium*, 5.
[142] SECOND VATICAN COUNCIL, Pastoral Constitution *Gaudium et Spes*, 2b.

porary cultures and with the aspirations and problems of his times. In this context, indeed, he is called to be a living sign of Christ the Servant and to assume the Church's responsibility of "reading the signs of the time and of interpreting them in the light of the Gospel, so that, in language intelligible to every generation, she may be able to answer the ever-recurring questions which men ask about this present life and of the life to come and how one is related to the other".[143]

Vocation to holiness

Sacramental basis

44. The universal call to holiness has its origin in the "baptism of faith" by which all are "truly made sons of God and sharers in the divine nature and thus are made holy".[144]

By the Sacrament of Holy Orders, deacons receive a "a new consecration to God" through which they are "anointed by the Holy Spirit and sent by Christ"[145] to serve God's people and "build up the Body of Christ" (*Eph* 4:12).

From this stems the *diaconal spirituality* with its source in what the Second Vatican Council calls "the sacramental grace of the diaconate".[146] In addition to helping the deacon to fulfil his functions this also affects his deepest being, imbuing it with a willingness to give his entire self over to the service of the Kingdom of God in the Church. As is indicated by the term "diaconate" itself, what characterizes the inner

---

[143] SECOND VATICAN COUNCIL, Pastoral Constitution *Gaudium et Spes*, 4a.
[144] SECOND VATICAN COUNCIL, Dogmatic Constitution *Lumen Gentium*, 40.
[145] SECOND VATICAN COUNCIL, Decree *Presbyterorum Ordinis*, 12a.
[146] SECOND VATICAN COUNCIL, Decree *Ad Gentes*, 16.

feelings and desire of those who receive the sacrament, is the *spirit of service*. Through the diaconate, what Jesus said of his mission is continually realized: "The Son of Man did not come to be served but to serve and to give his life as a ransom for many" (*Mt* 20:28).[147] Thus, through his ministry, the deacon lives the virtue of obedience: in faithfully carrying out those duties assigned to him, the deacon serves the episcopate and the presbyterate in the *munera* of Christ's mission and what he does is truly pastoral ministry, for the good of the faithful.

45.   Hence, the deacon should accept with gratitude the invitation to follow Christ the Servant and devote himself to it throughout the diverse circumstances of life. The character received in ordination conforms to Christ to whom the deacon should adhere ever more closely.

A binding requirement

Sanctification is a duty binding all the faithful.[148] For the deacon it has a further basis in the special consecration received.[149] It includes the practice of the Christian virtues and the various evangelical precepts and counsels according to one's own state of life. The deacon is called to live a holy life because he has been sanctified by the Holy Spirit in the sacraments of Baptism and Holy Orders and has been constitut-

---

[147] JOHN PAUL II, Catechesis at the General Audience of 20 October 1993, n. 1: *Insegnamenti*, XVI, 2 (1993), p. 1053.

[148] "All of Christ's faithful, each according to his or her own condition, must make a wholehearted effort to lead a holy life and to promote the growth of the Church and its continual sanctification" (*CIC*, canon 210).

[149] These "being at the service of the ministers of Christ and of the Church must keep themselves from all vice and be pleasing to God and dedicate themselves to those works considered good in the sight of man" (cf. *1 Tit* 3; 8-18 and 12-13): SECOND VATICAN COUNCIL, Dogmatic Constitution *Lumen Gentium*, 41; Cf. also PAUL VI, Apostolic Letter *Sacrum Diaconatus Ordinem*, VI, 25: *l.c.,* 702.

ed by the same Spirit a minister of Christ's Church to serve and sanctify mankind.[150]

For deacons the call to holiness means "following Jesus by an attitude of humble service which finds expression not only in works of charity but also in imbuing and forming thoughts and actions".[151] When "their ministry is consistent with this spirit (deacons) clearly highlight that quality which best shows the face of Christ: service [152] which makes one not only 'servants of God' but also servants of God in our own brethren".[153]

The Relations of Holy Order

Holy Order is essentially relational

46. By a special sacramental gift, Holy Order confers on the deacon a particular participation in the consecration and mission of Him who became servant of the Father for the redemption of mankind, and inserts him in a new and specific way in the mystery of Christ, of his Church and the salvation of all mankind. Hence the spiritual life of the deacon should deepen this threefold relationship by developing a community spirituality which bears witness to that communion essential to the nature of the Church.

Reference to Christ

47. The primary and most fundamental relationship must be with Christ, who assumed the condition of a

---

[150] "Clerics have a special obligation to seek holiness in their lives because they are consecrated to God by a new title through the reception of orders, and they are stewards of the mysteries of God in the service of His people" (*CIC,* canon 276, § 1).

[151] JOHN PAUL II, Catechesis at the General Audience of 20 October 1993, n. 2: *Insegnamenti,* XVI, 2 (1993), p. 1054.

[152] JOHN PAUL II, Catechesis at the General Audience of 20 October 1993, n. 1. *Insegnamenti,* XVI, 2 (1993), p. 1054.

[153] JOHN PAUL II, Catechesis at the General Audience of 20 October 1993, n. 1: *Insegnamenti,* XVI, 2 (1993), p. 1054.

slave for love of the Father and mankind.[154] In virtue of ordination the deacon is truly called to act in conformity with Christ the Servant.

The eternal Son of the Father "emptied himself assuming the form of a slave" (*Phil* 2:7) and lived this condition in obedience to the Father (*John* 4:34) and in humble service to the brethren (*John* 13:4-15). As servant of the Father in the work of salvation Christ constitutes the way, the truth and the life for every deacon in the Church.

All ministerial activity is meaningful when it leads to knowing, loving and following Christ in his diaconia. Thus deacons should strive to model their lives on Christ, who redeemed mankind by his obedience to the Father, an obedience "unto death, death on a cross" (*Phil* 2:8).

48. Indissolubly associated with this fundamental relationship with Christ is the Church [155] which Christ loves, purifies, nourishes and cares for (cf. *Eph* 5, 25:29). The deacon cannot live his configuration to Christ faithfully without sharing His love for the Church "for which he cannot but have a deep attachment because of her mission and her divine institution".[156]

Reference to the Church

The Rite of Ordination illustrates the connection which comes about between the bishop and the deacon: the bishop alone imposes hands on the candidate and invokes the outpouring of the Holy Spirit on him. Every deacon, therefore, finds the point of

---

[154] JOHN PAUL II allocution of 6 March 1985, n. 2: *Insegnamenti*, VIII, 1 (1985), p. 649. Post Synodal Apostolic Exhortation *Pastores Dabo Vobis*, 3, 21: *l.c.*, 661, 688.

[155] Cf. JOHN PAUL II, Post-Synodal Apostolic Exhortation *Pastores Dabo Vobis*, 16: *l.c.*, 681.

[156] JOHN PAUL II, Catechesis at the General Audience of 20 October 1993, n. 2: *Insegnamenti*, XVI, 2 (1993), p. 1055.

reference for his own ministry in hierarchical communion with the bishop.[157]

Diaconal ordination also underlines another ecclesial aspect: it communicates a ministerial sharing in Christ's *diaconia* with which God's people, governed by the Successor of Peter and those Bishops in communion with him, and in co-operation with the presbyterate, continues to serve the work of redemption. Deacons, therefore, are called to nourish themselves and their ministry with an ardent love for the Church, and a sincere desire for communion with the Holy Father, their own bishops and the priests of their dioceses.

Reference to the salvation of man in Christ

49. It must not be forgotten that the object of Christ's diaconia is mankind.[158] Every human being carries the traces of sin but is called to communion with God. "God so loved the world that He gave His only Son, so that all who believe in Him might not die but have eternal life" (*John* 3:16). It was for this plan of love, that Christ became a slave and took human flesh. The Church continues to be the sign and instrument of that diaconia in history.

In virtue of the Sacrament of Orders deacons are at the service of their brothers and sisters needing of salvation. As mankind can see the fullness of the Father's love by which they are saved in the words and deeds of Christ the Servant, so too this same charity must be apparent in the life of the deacon. Growth in imitation of Christ's love for mankind — which surpasses all ideologies — is thus an essential component of the spiritual life of every deacon.

---

[157] Cf. PAUL VI, Apostolic Letter *Sacrum Diaconatus Ordinem*, V, 23: *l.c.*, 702.

[158] Cf. JOHN PAUL II, Encyclical Letter *Redemptor Hominis* (4 March 1979), nn 13-17: *AAS* 71 (1979), pp. 282-300.

A "natural inclination of service to the sacred hierarchy and to the Christian community" [159] is required of those who seek admission to the diaconate. This should not be understood "in the sense of a simple spontaneity of natural disposition...it is rather an inclination of nature inspired by grace, with a spirit of service that conforms human behaviour to Christ's. The sacrament of the diaconate develops this inclination: it makes the subject to share more closely in Christ's spirit of service and imbues the will with a special grace so that in all his actions he will be motivated by a *new inclination* to serve his brothers and sisters". [160]

Aids to the Spiritual Life

50. The aforementioned points of reference emphasize the primacy of the spiritual life. The deacon, mindful that the diaconia of Christ surpasses all natural capacities, should continually commit himself in conscience and in freedom to His invitation: "Remain in me and I in you. As the branch cannot bear fruit unless it remain in the vine, so also with you unless you remain in me" (*John* 15:4).

Primacy of the Spiritual Life

Following Christ in the diaconate is an attractive but difficult undertaking. While it brings satisfaction and rewards, it can also be open to the difficulties and trials experienced by the followers of the Lord Jesus Christ. In order to live this ministry to the full, deacons must know Christ intimately so that He may shoulder the burdens of their ministry. They must give priority to the spiritual life and live their diaco-

[159] PAUL VI, Apostolic Letter *Sacrum Diaconatus Ordinem*, II, 8: *l.c.,* 700.

[160] JOHN PAUL II, Catechesis at the General Audience of 20 October 1993, n. 2: *Insegnamenti*, XVI, 2 (1993), p. 1054.

nia with generosity. They should organize their ministry and their professional and, when married, family obligations, so as to grow in their commitment to the person and mission of Christ the Servant.

Ministry   51.   Progress in the spiritual life is achieved primarily by faithful and tireless exercise of the ministry in integrity of life.[161] Such ministry not only develops the spiritual life but promotes the theological virtues, a disposition to selflessness, service to the brethren and hierarchical communion. What has been said of priests, *mutatis mutandis*, also applies to deacons: "Through the sacred actions they perform every day....they are set on the right course to perfection of life. The very holiness of priests is of the greatest benefit for the fruitful fulfilment of their ministry".[162]

The spirituality of the ministry of the word   52.   The deacon should always be mindful of the exhortation made to him in the Rite of Ordination: "Receive the Gospel of Christ of which you are the herald; believe what you preach, teach what you believe and put into practice what you teach".[163] For a worthy and fruitful proclamation of the word of God, deacons should "immerse themselves in the Scriptures by constant sacred reading and diligent study. For it must not happen that anybody becomes 'an empty preacher of the word of God to others, not being a hearer of the word in his own heart'[164] when he should be sharing the boundless riches of the divine

---

[161] Cf. SECOND VATICAN COUNCIL, Decree *Presbyterorum Ordinis*, nn. 14 & 15: *CIC*, canon 276, § 2, n. 1°.

[162] SECOND VATICAN COUNCIL, Decree *Presbyterorum Ordinis*, 12.

[163] *Pontificale Romanum - De Ordinatione Episcopi, presbyterorum et diaconorum*, n. 210; ed. cit., p. 125.

[164] St Augustine, *Sermones*, 179, 1: *PL* 38, 966.

word with the faithful committed to his care, especially in the sacred Liturgy".[165]

Moreover, deacons, under the guidance of those in the Church who are true teachers of divine and Catholic truth,[166] should strive to deepen their knowledge of the word, so as to hear its call and experience its saving power (cf. *Rom* 1:16). Their sanctification is based on their consecration and on their mission. This is true also with regard to the word and they should be conscious that they are its ministers. As members of the hierarchy, the actions and public pronouncements of deacons involve the Church. Consequently, it is essential for pastoral charity that deacons should ensure the authenticity of their own teaching. Likewise, in the spirit of the profession of faith and the oath of fidelity,[167] taken prior to ordination, they should preserve their own clear and effective communion with the Holy Father, the episcopal order and with their own bishops, not only with regard to the articles of the Creed, but also with regard to the teaching of ordinary Magisterium and the Church's discipline. Indeed, "such is the force and power of the word of God that it can serve the Church as her support and vigour, and the children of God for their strength, food for the soul, and for a pure and lasting fount of spiritual life".[168] The closer deacons come to the word of God, therefore, the greater

---

[165] SECOND VATICAN COUNCIL, Dogmatic Constitution *Dei Verbum* 25; cf. PAUL VI, Apostolic Letter *Sacrum Diaconatus Ordinem*, VI, 26, 1; *l.c.,* 703; *CIC,* canon 276, § 2, n. 2°.

[166] Cf. SECOND VATICAN COUNCIL, Dogmatic Constitution *Lumen Gentium,* 25a.

[167] Cf. *CIC,* canon 833; CONGREGATION FOR THE DOCTRINE OF THE FAITH, Professio fidei et iusiurandum fidelitatis in suscipiendo officio nomine Ecclesiae exercendo: *AAS* 81 (1989), pp. 104-106 and 1169.

[168] SECOND VATICAN COUNCIL, Dogmatic Constitution *Dei Verbum,* 21.

will be their desire to communicate it to their brothers and sisters. God speaks to man in Sacred Scripture: [169] by his preaching, the sacred minister fosters this salvific encounter. Then, lest the faithful be deprived of the word of God through the ignorance or indolence of its ministers, deacons should devote themselves to preach the word tirelessly and yet be mindful that the exercise of the ministry of the word is not confined to preaching alone.

Spirituality of the ministry of the liturgy

53. Likewise, when the deacon baptizes or distributes the Body and Blood of Christ or serves at the celebration of the other sacraments and sacramentals, he confirms his identity in the Church: he is a minister of the Body of Christ, both mystical and ecclesial. Let him remember that, when lived with faith and reverence, these actions of the Church contribute much to growth in the spiritual life and to the increase of the Christian community. [170]

The Sacraments

54. With regard to the spiritual life, deacons should devote particular importance to the sacraments of grace whose purpose "is to sanctify men, to build up the Body of Christ, and finally to give worship to God". [171]

Above all, they should participate with particular faith at the daily celebration of the eucharistic sacrifice, [172] possibly exercising their own proper liturgical *munus*, and adore the Lord, present in the Sacra-

---

[169] Cf. SECOND VATICAN COUNCIL, Constitution *Sacrosanctum Concilium*, 7.

[170] Cf. SECOND VATICAN COUNCIL, Constitution *Sacrosanctum Concilium*, 7.

[171] SECOND VATICAN COUNCIL, Constitution *Sacrosanctum Concilium*, 59a.

[172] Cf. *CIC*, canon 276, § 2, n. 2; PAUL VI, Apostolic Letter *Sacrum Diaconatus Ordinem*, VI, 26, 2: *l.c.*, 703.

ment,[173] because in the Blessed Eucharist, source and summit of all evangelization, "the whole spiritual good of the Church is contained".[174] In the Blessed Eucharist they truly encounter Christ who, for love of man, became an expiatory victim, the food of life eternal and friend of all who suffer.

Conscious of his own weakness and trusting the mercy of God the deacon should regularly approach the Sacrament of Penance,[175] in which sinful man encounters Christ the Redeemer, receives forgiveness of sin and is impelled towards the fullness of charity.

55. In performing the works of charity entrusted to them by their bishops, deacons should always be guided by the love of Christ for all men instead of personal interests and ideologies which are injurious to the universality of salvation or deny the transcendent vocation of man. They should be ever conscious that the diaconia of charity necessarily leads to a growth of communion within the particular Churches since charity is the very soul of ecclesial communion. Deacons are thus obliged to foster fraternity and cooperation with the priests of their dioceses and sincere communion with their bishops. *Spirituality of the ministry of charity*

56. The deacon shall always remain faithful to the Lord's command: "But watch at all times, praying that you may have strength to escape all these things that will take place, and to stand before the Son of man" (*Lk* 21:36 cf. *Phil* 4:6-7). *Prayer life*

---

[173] Cf. PAUL VI, Apostolic Letter *Sacrum Diaconatus Ordinem*, VI, 26, 2: *l.c.,* 703.

[174] SECOND VATICAN COUNCIL, Decree *Presbyterorum Ordinis*, 5b.

[175] Cf. canon 276, § 2, n. 5°; PAUL VI, Apostolic Letter *Sacrum Diaconatus Ordinem*, VI, 26, 3: *l.c.,* 703.

Prayer, which is a personal dialogue with God, confers the strength needed to follow Christ and serve the brethren. In the light of this certainty, deacons should form themselves according to the various types of prayer: the celebration of the Liturgy of the Hours, as prescribed by the various Episcopal Conferences,[176] should inform their whole prayer life since deacons, as ministers, intercede for the entire Church. Such prayer is carried over into the *lectio divina*, arduous mental prayer and the spiritual retreat prescribed by particular law.[177]

The habit of penance should also be taken to heart together with other means of sanctification which foster personal encounter with God.[178]

Love for the Church and the Blessed Virgin Mary

57. Participation in the mystery of Christ the Servant necessarily directs the deacon's heart to the Church and her most holy Mother. Christ indeed cannot be separated from the Church which is his Body. True union with Christ the Head cannot but foster true love for His body which is the Church. This love will commit the deacon to work diligently to build up the Church by faithful discharge of his ministerial duties, through fraternity and hierarchical communion with his own bishop and with the presbyterate. The deacon should be concerned for the entire Church: the universal Church, the principle and perpetually visible foundation of whose unity is the Roman Pontiff, the Successor of St Peter,[179] as well as the particular Church which "adhering to its pastor and united by him in the Holy

---

[176] Cf. *CIC,* canon 276, § 2, n. 3°.
[177] Cf. *CIC,* canon 276, § 2, n. 4°.
[178] Cf. *CIC,* canon 276, § 2, n. 5°.
[179] SECOND VATICAN COUNCIL, Dogmatic Constitution *Lumen Gentium,* 23a.

Spirit through the Gospel and the Eucharist.... in which the one, holy, Catholic and apostolic Church of Christ is present.[180]

Love for Christ and for His Church is profoundly linked to love of the Blessed Virgin Mary, handmaid of the Lord. With her unique title of Mother, she was the selfless helper of her divine Son's diaconia (cf. *John* 19:25-27). Love of the Mother of God, based on faith and expressed in daily recitation of the Rosary, imitation of her virtues and trust in her, are indeed signs of authentic filial devotion.[181]

With deep veneration and affection Mary looks on every deacon. Indeed, "the creature who more than any other who has lived the full truth of vocation is Mary the Virgin Mother, and she did so in intimate communion with Christ: no one has responded with a love greater than hers to the immense love of God".[182] This love of the Virgin Mary, handmaid of the Lord, which is born and rooted in the word, will cause deacons to imitate her life. In this way a Marian dimension is introduced into the Church which is very close to the vocation of the deacon.[183]

58. Regular spiritual direction is truly of the greatest assistance to deacons. Experience clearly shows how much can be gained in sincere and

Spiritual direction

---

[180] SECOND VATICAN COUNCIL, Decree *Christus Dominus*, 11; *CIC*, canon 369.

[181] Cf. *CIC*, canon 276, § 2, n. 5°; PAUL VI, Apostolic Letter *Sacrum Diaconatus Ordinem*, VI, 26, 4: *l.c.*, 703.

[182] JOHN PAUL II, Post-Synodal Apostolic Exhortation *Pastores Dabo Vobis*, 36, quoting *Propositio* 5 of the Synodal fathers: *l.c.*, 718.

[183] Cf. JOHN PAUL II, Allocution to the Roman Curia, 22 December 1987: *AAS* 80 (1988), pp. 1025-1034; Apostolic Letter *Mulieris Dignitatem*, 27: *AAS* 80 (1988), p. 1718.

humble dialogue with a wise spiritual director, not only in the resolution of doubts and problems which inevitably arise throughout life, but also in employing the necessary discernment to arrive at better self-knowledge and to grow in faithful fellowship of Christ.

Spirituality of deacons and states of life

Unity in diversity

59.   In contrast with the requirement for the priesthood, not only celibate men, in the first place and widowers, may be admitted to the permanent Diaconate but also men who live in the Sacrament of Matrimony.[184]

Celibate deacons

60.   With gratitude, the Church recognises the gift of celibacy which God gives to some of her members and, in different ways, both in the East and West, she has linked it to the ordained ministry with which it is always particularly consonant.[185] The Church is conscious that this gift, accepted and lived for the sake of the Kingdom of God (cf. Mt 19:12), directs the whole person of the deacon towards Christ who devoted Himself in chastity to the service of the Father so as to bring man to the fullness of the Kingdom. Loving God and serving the brethren by this complete choice, so far from impeding the personal development of deacons, fosters man's true perfection which is found in charity. In celibate life, indeed, love becomes a sign of total and undivided consecration to Christ and of greater freedom to serve God

---

[184] Cf. SECOND VATICAN COUNCIL, Dogmatic Constitution *Lumen Gentium*, 29b.

[185] His rationibus in mysteriis Christi Eiusque missione fundatis, coelibatus ...omnibus ad Ordinem sacrum promovendis lege impositum est": SECOND VATICAN COUNCIL, Decree *Presbyterorum Ordinis*, 16; cf. *CIC,* canon 247, § 1; canon 277, § 1, canon 1037.

and man.[186] The choice of celibacy is not an expression of contempt for marriage nor of flight from reality but a special way of serving man and the world.

Contemporary man, very often submerged in the ephemeral, is particularly sensitive to those who are a living witness of the eternal. Hence, deacons should be especially careful to give witness to their brothers and sisters by their fidelity to the celibate life the better to move them to seek those values consonant with man's transcendent vocation. "Celibacy 'for the sake of the Kingdom' is not only an eschatological sign. It also has a great social significance in contemporary life for service to the People of God".[187]

In order to conserve this special gift of God throughout life for the benefit of the entire Church, deacons should not depend excessively on their own resources, but should be faithful to the spiritual life and the duties of their ministry in a spirit of prudence and vigilance, remembering that "the spirit is willing but the flesh is weak" (*Mt* 26:41).

They should be particularly careful in their relationships with others lest familiarity create difficulties for continence or give rise to scandal.[188]

They must finally be aware that in contemporary society, it is necessary to exercise careful discernment when using the means of social communications.

61. The Sacrament of Matrimony sanctifies conjugal love and constitutes it a sign of the love with which Christ gives himself to the Church (cf. Eph. 5:25). It is a gift from God and should be a source of nour-

Married Deacons

---

[186] Cf. *CIC,* canon 277, § 1; SECOND VATICAN COUNCIL, Decree *Optatam Totius,* 10.

[187] JOHN PAUL II, Letter to Priests on Holy Thursday, 8 April 1979, 8: *AAS* 71 (1979), p. 408.

[188] Cf. canon 277, § 2.

ishment for the spiritual life of those deacons who are married. Since family life and professional responsibilities must necessarily reduce the amount of time which married deacons can dedicate to the ministry, it will be necessary to integrate these various elements in a unitary fashion, especially by means of shared prayer. In marriage, love becomes an interpersonal giving of self, a mutual fidelity, a source of new life, a support in times of joy and sorrow: in short, love becomes service. When lived in faith, this *family service* is for the rest of the faithful an example of the love of Christ. The married deacon must use it as a stimulus of his diaconia in the Church.

Married deacons should feel especially obliged to give clear witness to the sanctity of marriage and the family. The more they grow in mutual love, the greater their dedication to their children and the more significant their example for the Christian community. "The nurturing and deepening of mutual, sacrificial love between husband and wife constitutes perhaps the most significant involvement of a deacon's wife in her husband's public ministry in the Church".[189] This love grows thanks to chastity which flourishes, even in the exercise of paternal responsibilities, by respect for spouses and the practice of a certain continence. This virtue fosters a mutual self-giving which soon becomes evident in ministry. It eschews possessive behaviour, undue pursuit of professional success and the incapacity to programme time. Instead, it promotes authentic interpersonal relationships, OIC, and the capacity to see everything in its proper perspective.

Special care should be taken to ensure that the families of deacons be made aware of the demands of

---

[189] JOHN PAUL II, Allocution to the permanent deacons of the U.S.A. in Detroit (19 September 1987), n. 5: *Insegnamenti*, X, 3 (1987), p. 658.

the diaconal ministry. The spouses of married deacons, who must give their consent to their husband's decision to seek ordination to the diaconate,[190] should be assisted to play their role with joy and discretion. They should esteem all that concerns the Church, especially the duties assigned to their husbands. For this reason it is opportune that they should be kept duly informed of their husbands' activities in order to arrive at an harmonious balance between family, professional and ecclesial responsibilities. In the children of married deacons, where such is possible, an appreciation of their father's ministry can also be fostered. They in turn should be involved in the apostolate and give coherent witness in their lives.

In conclusion, the families of married deacons, as with all Christian families, are called to participate actively and responsibly in the Church's mission in the contemporary world. "In particular the deacon and his wife must be a living example of *fidelity and indissolubility in Christian marriage* before a world which is in dire need of such signs. By facing in a *spirit of faith* the challenges of married life and the demands of daily living, they strengthen the family life not only of the Church community but of the whole of society. They also show how the obligations of family life, work and ministry can be harmonized *in the service* of the Church's mission. Deacons and their wives and children can be a great encouragement to others who are working to promote family life".[191]

62.   It is necessary to reflect on the situation of the deacon following the death of his wife. This is a particular moment in life which calls for faith and Christian hope. The loss of a spouse should not destroy

Deacons who are widowers

---

[190] Cf. *CIC,* canon 1031, § 2.
[191] JOHN PAUL II, Allocution to the permanent deacons of the USA in Detroit, 19 September 1987, n. 5; *Insegnamenti,* X, 3 (1987), pp. 658-659.

dedication to the rearing of children nor lead to hopelessness. While this period of life is difficult, it is also an opportunity for interior purification and an impetus for growth in charity and service to one's children and to all the members of the Church. It is a call to grow in hope since faithful discharge of the ministry is a way of reaching Christ and those in the Father's glory who are dear to us.

It must be recognised, however, that the loss of a spouse gives rise to a new situation in a family which profoundly influences personal relationships and in many instances can give rise to economic difficulties. With great charity, therefore, widowed deacons should be helped to discern and accept their new personal circumstances and to persevere in providing for their children and the new needs of their families.

In particular, the widowed deacon should be supported in living perfect and perpetual continence.[192] He should be helped to understand the profound ecclesial reasons which preclude his remarriage (cf. 1 Tim 3:12), in accordance with the constant discipline of the Church in the East and West.[193] This can be achieved through an intensification of one's dedication to others for the love of God in the ministry. In such cases the fraternal assistance of other ministers, of the faithful and of the bishop can be most comforting to widowed deacons.

With regard to the widows of deacons, care should be taken, where possible, by the clergy and the faithful to ensure that they are never neglected and that their needs are provided for.

---

[192] Cf. *CIC*, canon 277, § 1.
[193] PAUL VI, Apostolic Letter *Sacrum Diaconatus Ordinem*, III, 16: *l.c.*, 701: Apostolic Letter *Ad Pascendum*, VI: *l.c.*, 539; *CIC*, canon 1087. Provision is made for possible exceptions to this discipline in the circular letter of the Congregation for Divine Worship and the Discipline of the Sacraments, N. 263/97, of 6 June 1997, n. 8.

4

CONTINUING FORMATION OF DEACONS

Characteristics

63. The continuing formation of deacons is a human necessity which must be seen in continuity with the divine call to serve the Church in the ministry and with the initial formation given to deacons, to the extent that these are considered two initial moments in a single, living, process of Christian and diaconal life.[194] Indeed, "those who are ordained to the diaconate are obliged to ongoing doctrinal formation which perfects and completes what they received prior to ordination",[195] so that, by a periodic renewal of the "I am" pronounced by deacons at their ordination, the vocation "to" the diaconate continues and finds expression as vocation "in" the diaconate. On the part of both the Church which provides ongoing formation and of deacons who are its recipients, such formation should be regarded as a mutual obligation and duty arising from the nature of the vocational commitment which has been assumed.

The continuing need to provide and receive adequate, integral formation is an indispensable obligation for both bishops and deacons.

---

[194] JOHN PAUL II, Post-Synodal Apostolic Exhortation, *Pastores Dabo Vobis*, n. 42.

[195] JOHN PAUL II, Catechesis at the General Audience of 20 October 1993, n. 4: *Insegnamenti*, XVI, 2 (1993), p. 1056.

Ecclesiastical norms regarding ongoing formation [196] have constantly emphasised the obligatory nature of such formation for the apostolic life and stressed the need for it to be global, interdisciplinary, profound, scientific and propedeutic. Application of these norms is all the more necessary in those instances where initial formation did not adhere to the ordinary model.

Continuing formation should be informed with the characteristics of fidelity to Christ, to the Church and to "continuing conversion" which is a fruit of sacramental grace articulated in the pastoral charity proper to every moment of ordained ministry. This formation is similar to the fundamental choice, which must be reaffirmed and renewed throughout the permanent diaconate by a long series of coherent responses which are based on and animated by the initial acceptance of the ministry. [197]

Motivation

Connection with the ministry

64. Inspired by the prayer of ordination, ongoing formation is based on the need of every deacon to love Christ in such manner as to imitate him ("may they be images of your Son"). It seeks to confirm him in uncompromising fidelity to a personal vocation to ministry ("may they fulfil faithfully the works of the ministry") and proposes a radical, sincere following of Christ the Servant ("may the example of their

---

[196] PAUL VI, Apostolic Letter *Sacrum Diaconatus Ordinem*, II, 8-10; III, 14-15: *l.c.,* 699-701; Apostolic Letter *Ad Pascendum*, VII: *l.c.,* 540; *CIC,* canons 236, 1027, 1032 § 3.

[197] Cf. JOHN PAUL II, Post-Synodal Apostolic Exhortation *Pastores Dabo Vobis*, 70: *l.c.,* 780.

lives be a constant reminder of the Gospel... may they be sincere...solicitous...and vigilant").

The basis and motivation of this formation, therefore, "is the dynamism of the order itself",[198] while its nourishment is the Holy Eucharist, compendium of the entire Christian ministry and endless source of every spiritual energy. St Paul's exhortation to Timothy can also be applied, in a certain sense, to deacons: "I remind you to fan into a flame the gift of God that you have" (2 Tim 1:6; cf. 1 Tim 4:14-16). The theological demands of their call to a singular ministry of ecclesial service requires of them a growing love for the Church, shown forth by their faithful carrying out of their proper functions and responsibilities. Chosen by God to be holy, serving the Church and all mankind, the deacon should continually grow in awareness of his own ministerial character in a manner that is balanced, responsible, solicitous and always joyful.

Subjects

65. From the perspective of the deacon, primary protagonist and primary subject of the obligation, ongoing formation is first and foremost a process of continual conversion. It embraces every aspect of his person as deacon, that is to say, consecrated by the Sacrament of Order and placed at the service of the Church, and seeks to develop all of his potential. This enables him to live to the full the ministerial gifts that he has received in diverse circumstances of time and place and in the tasks assigned to him by the bishop.[199] The solicitude of the Church for the permanent formation of deacons

Deacons

---

[198] JOHN PAUL II, Post-Synodal Apostolic Exhortation *Pastores Dabo Vobis*, 70: *l.c.,* 779.

[199] JOHN PAUL II, Post-Synodal Apostolic Exhortation *Pastores Dabo Vobis*, 76; 79: *l.c.,* 793; 796.

would, however, be ineffective without their co-operation and commitment. Thus formation cannot be reduced merely to participating at courses or study days or other such activities: it calls for every deacon to be aware of the need for ongoing formation and to cultivate it with interest and in a spirit of healthy initiative. Books approved by ecclesiastical authority should be chosen as material for reading; periodicals known for their fidelity to the Magisterium should be followed; time should be set aside for daily meditation. Constant self-formation which helps him to serve the Church ever better is an important part of the service asked of every deacon.

Formators 66. From the perspective of the bishops [200] (and their fellow workers in the presbyterate), who bear responsibility for formation, ongoing formation consists in helping the deacon to overcome any dualism that might exist between spirituality and ministry and, more fundamentally, any dichotomy between their civil profession and diaconal spirituality and "respond generously to the commitment demanded by the dignity and the responsibility which God conferred upon them through the sacrament of Orders; in guarding, defending, and developing their specific identity and vocation; and in sanctifying themselves and others through the exercise of their ministry". [201]

Both dimensions are complementary and reciprocal since they are founded, with the help of supernatural gifts, in the interior unity of the person.

The assistance which formators are called to offer deacons will be successful in as much as it responds

---

[200] Cf. SECOND VATICAN COUNCIL, Decree *Christus Dominus*, 15; JOHN PAUL II, Post-Synodal Apostolic Exhortation *Pastores Dabo Vobis*, 79: *l.c.*, 797.

[201] CONGREGATION FOR THE CLERGY, *Tota Ecclesia*, Directory for the ministry and life of priests (31 January 1994), n. 71: p. 76.

to the personal needs of each deacon, since every deacon lives his ministry in the Church as a unique person placed in particular circumstances.

Personalized assistance to deacons also assures them of that love with which mother Church is close to them as they strive to live faithfully the sacramental grace of their calling. It is thus of supreme importance that each deacon be able to choose a spiritual director, approved by the bishop, with whom he can have regular and frequent contact.

The entire diocesan community is also, in some sense, involved in the formation of deacons.[202] This is particularly true of the parish priest or other priests charged with formation who should personally support them with fraternal solicitude.

Specificity

67. Personal concern and commitment in ongoing formation are unequivocal signs of a coherent response to divine vocation, of sincere love for the Church and of authentic pastoral zeal for the Christian faithful and all men. What has been said of priests can also be applied to deacons: "ongoing formation is a necessary means of reaching the object of one's vocation which is service of God and one's people".[203]

Ongoing ministerial formation

It must be seen in continuity with initial formation since it pursues the same ends as initial formation and seeks to integrate, conserve and deepen what was begun in initial formation.

---

[202] Cf. JOHN PAUL II, Post-Synodal Apostolic Exhortation *Pastores Dabo Vobis*, 78: *l.c.*, 795.

[203] CONGREGATION FOR THE CLERGY, Directory for the ministry and life of priests *Tota Ecclesia*, 71: p. 76.

The essential availability of the deacon to others is a practical expression of sacramental configuration to Christ the Servant, received through ordination and indelibly impressed upon the soul. It is a permanent reminder to the deacon in his life and ministry. Hence permanent formation cannot be reduced merely to complementary education or to a form of training in better *techniques*. Ongoing formation cannot be confined simply to updating, but should seek to facilitate a practical configuration of the deacon's entire life to Christ who loves all and serves all.

Dimensions

Complete formation

68.   Ongoing formation must include and harmonize all dimensions of the life and ministry of the deacon. Thus, as with the permanent formation of priests, it should be complete, systematic and personalized in its diverse aspects whether human, spiritual, intellectual or pastoral.[204]

Human formation

69.   As in the past, attention to the various aspects of the human formation of deacons is an important task for Pastors. The deacon, aware that he is chosen as a man among men to be at the service of the salvation of all, should be open to being helped in developing his human qualities as valuable instruments for ministry. He should strive to perfect all those aspects of his personality which might render his ministry more effective.

To fulfil successfully his vocation to holiness and his particular ecclesial mission, he should, above all,

---

[204] Cf. JOHN PAUL II, Post-Synodal Apostolic Exhortation, *Pastores Dabo Vobis,* 71: *l.c.,* 783; CONGREGATION FOR THE CLERGY, Directory for the ministry and life of priests, *Tota Ecclesia,* n. 74, p. 78.

fix his gaze on Him who is true God and true man
and practice the natural and supernatural virtues
which conform him more closely to the image of
Christ and make him worthy of the respect of the
faithful.[205] In their ministry and daily life particularly,
deacons should foster in themselves kind-heartedness,
patience, affability, strength of character, zeal for justice, fidelity to promises given, a spirit of sacrifice
and consistency with tasks freely undertaken. The
practice of these virtues will assist in arriving at a
balanced personality, maturity and discernment.

Conscious of the example of integrity in his social
activity, the deacon should reflect on his ability to dialogue, on correctness in human relationships and on
cultural discernment. He should also give careful consideration to the value of friendship and to his treatment of others.[206]

70. Ongoing spiritual formation is closely connected *Spiritual*
with diaconal spirituality, which it must nourish and *formation*
develop, and with the ministry, which is sustained by
"a truly personal encounter with Jesus, a relationship
with the Father and a profound experience of the
Spirit".[207] Hence, deacons should be encouraged by
the Pastors of the Church to cultivate their spiritual
lives in a responsible manner, for it is from this life
that springs up that love which sustains their ministry

---

[205] Cf. St Ignatius of Antioch: "Deacons, who are ministers of
Christ Jesus, must be acceptable to all in every respect. They are
not servants of food and drink. They are ministers of the Church
of God" (*Epist. ad Trallianos*, 2, 3: F. X. Funk, *o.c.*, I, pp. 244-
245).

[206] Cf. John Paul II, Post-Synodal Apostolic Exhortation, *Pastores
Dabo Vobis*, 72: *l.c.*, 783; Congregation for the Clergy,
Directory for the ministry and life of priestly, *Tota Ecclesia*, 75,
ed. cit., pp. 75-76.

[207] John Paul II, Post-Synodal Apostolic Exhortation, *Pastores Dabo
Vobis*, 72: *l.c.*, 785.

and makes it fruitful, and prevents its reduction to mere "functionalism" or bureaucracy.

In particular, the spiritual formation of deacons should inculcate those attitudes related to the triple diaconia of word, liturgy and charity.

Assiduous meditation on Sacred Scripture will achieve familiarity and worshipful dialogue with the living God and thus an assimilation of the revealed word.

A profound knowledge of Tradition and of the liturgical books will help the deacon to discover continually the riches of the divine mysteries and thus become their worthy minister. A solicitude for fraternal charity will impel him to practice the spiritual and corporal works of mercy, and provide living signs of the Church's love.

All of this requires careful planning and organization of time and resources. Improvisation should be avoided. In addition to spiritual direction, deacons should try to pursue study courses on the great themes of the theological tradition of Christian spirituality, intensive sessions in spirituality and pilgrimages to places of spiritual interest.

While on retreat, which should be at least every other year,[208] deacons should work out a spiritual programme which they should periodically share with their spiritual directors. This programme should include a period of daily eucharistic adoration and provide for exercises of Marian devotion, liturgical prayer, personal meditation and the habitual ascetical practices.

The centre of this spiritual itinerary must be the Holy Eucharist since it is the touchstone of the dea-

---

[208] Cf. PAUL VI, Apostolic Letter *Sacrum Diaconatus Ordinem*, VI, 28: *l.c.,* 703; *CIC,* canon 276, § 4.

con's life and activity, the indispensable means of perseverance, the criterion of authentic renewal and of a balanced synthesis of life. In this way, the spiritual formation of the deacon will reveal the Holy Eucharist as Passover, in its annual articulation in Holy Week, in its weekly articulation on Sunday and in its constant articulation at daily Mass.

71.   The insertion of deacons into the mystery of the Church, in virtue of Baptism and their reception of the first grade of the Sacrament of Orders, requires that ongoing formation strengthen in them the consciousness and willingness to live in intelligent, active and mature communion with their bishops and the priests of their dioceses, and with the Supreme Pontiff who is the visible foundation of the entire Church's unity. *Formation in ecclesial communion*

When formed in this way, they can become in their ministry effective promoters of communion. In situations of conflict they, in particular, should make every effort to restore peace for the good of the Church.

72.   The doctrine of the faith should be deepened by suitable initiatives such as study days, renewal courses and the frequentation of academic institutions. For the same reason, it would be particularly useful to promote careful, in-depth and systematic study of the *Catechism of the Catholic Church*. *Intellectual formation*

It is necessary that deacons have an accurate knowledge of the Sacraments of Holy Orders, the Holy Eucharist, Baptism and Matrimony. They must develop a knowledge of those aspects of philosophy, ecclesiology, dogmatic Theology, Sacred Scripture, and Canon Law which most assist them in their ministry.

Such courses, while aimed at theological renewal, should also lead to prayer, ecclesial communion and greater pastoral efforts in response to the urgent need for new evangelization.

Under sure guidance, the documents of the Magisterium should be studied in common, and in relation to the needs of the pastoral ministry, especially those documents in which the Church responds to the more pressing moral and doctrinal questions. Thus, with a sense of communion, deacons will be enabled to achieve and express due obedience to the Pastor of the universal Church and to diocesan bishops, as well as to promote fidelity to the doctrine and discipline of the Church.

In addition, it is of the greatest use and relevance to study, appropriate and diffuse the social doctrine of the Church. A good knowledge of that teaching will permit many deacons to mediate it in their different professions, at work and in their families. The diocesan bishop may also invite those who are capable to specialize in a theological discipline and obtain the necessary academic qualifications at those pontifical academies or institutes recognized by the Apostolic See which guarantee doctrinally correct formation.

Deacons should pursue systematic study not only to perfect their theological knowledge but also to revitalize constantly their ministry in view of the changing needs of the ecclesial community.

Pastoral formation   73. Together with study of the sacred sciences, appropriate measures should be taken to ensure that deacons acquire a pastoral methodology [209] for an effective ministry. Permanent pastoral formation consists, in the first place, in constantly encouraging the deacon to perfect the effectiveness of his ministry of making the love and service of Christ present in the

---

[209] Cf. *CIC,* canon 279.

Church and in society without distinction, especially to the poor and to those most in need. Indeed it is from the pastoral love of Christ that the ministry of deacons draws its model and inspiration. This same love urges the deacon, in collaboration with his bishop and the priests of his diocese, to promote the mission of the laity in the world. He will thus be a stimulus "to become ever better acquainted with the real situation of the men and women to whom he is sent, to discern the call of the Spirit in the historical circumstances in which he finds himself, and to seek the most suitable methods and the most useful forms for carrying out his ministry today",[210] in loyal and convinced communion with the Supreme Pontiff and with his own bishop.

The effectiveness of the apostolate sometimes calls also for group work requiring a knowledge and respect of the diversity and complementarity of the gifts and respective functions of priests, deacons and the lay faithful, within the organic nature of ecclesial communion.

Organization and means

74. The diversity of circumstances in the particular Churches makes it difficult to give an exhaustive account of how best to organize the suitable ongoing formation of permanent deacons. Yet it is necessary that all such formation be accomplished by means which accord with theological and pastoral clarity.

A few general criteria, easily applicable to diverse concrete circumstances, may be mentioned in this respect.

---

[210] JOHN PAUL II, Post-Synodal Apostolic Exhortation, *Pastores Dabo Vobis*, 72: *l.c.,* 783.

75. The primary locus of ongoing formation for deacons is the ministry itself. The deacon matures in its exercise and by focusing his own call to holiness on the fulfilment of his social and ecclesial duties, in particular, of his ministerial functions and responsibilities. The formation of deacons should, therefore, concentrate in a special way on awareness of their ministerial character.

76. Permanent formation must follow a well planned programme drawn up and approved by competent authority. It must be unitary, divided into progressive stages, and at the same time, in perfect harmony with the Magisterium of the Church. It is better that the programme should insist on a basic minimum to be followed by all deacons and which should be distinct from later specialization courses.

Programmes such as this should take into consideration two distinct but closely related levels of formation: the diocesan level, in reference to the bishop or his delegate, and the community level in which the deacon exercises his own ministry, in reference to the parish priest or some other priest.

77. The first appointment of a deacon to a parish or a pastoral area is a very sensitive moment. Introducing the deacon to those in charge of the community (the parish priest, priests), and the community to the deacon, helps them not only to come to know each other but contributes to a collaboration based on mutual respect and dialogue, in a spirit of faith and fraternal charity. The community into which a deacon comes can have a highly important formative effect, especially when he realizes the importance of respect for well proven traditions and knows how to listen, discern, serve and love as Jesus Christ did.

Deacons in their initial pastoral assignments should be carefully supervised by an exemplary priest especially appointed to this task by the bishop.

78. Periodic meetings should be arranged for deacons which treat of liturgical and spiritual matters, of continuous theological renewal and study, either at diocesan or supra-diocesan level.

Under the bishop's authority and without multiplying existent structures, periodic meeting should be arranged between priests, deacons, religious and laity involved in pastoral work both to avoid compartmentalization or the development of isolated groups and to guarantee co-ordinated unity for different pastoral activities.

The bishop should show particular solicitude for deacons since they are his collaborators. When possible he should attend their meetings and always ensure the presence of his representative.

79. With the approval of the diocesan bishop, a realistic programme of ongoing formation should be drawn up in accordance with the present dispositions, taking due account of factors such as the age and circumstances of deacons, together with the demands made on them by their pastoral ministry.

To accomplish this task, the bishop might constitute a group of suitable formators or seek the assistance of neighbouring dioceses.

80. It is desirable that the bishop set up a diocesan *organization for the co-ordination of deacons,* to plan, co-ordinate and supervise the diaconal ministry from the discernment of vocation,[211] to the exercise of ministry and formation — including ongoing formation.

---

[211] Cf. *CIC,* canon 1029.

This organization should be composed of the Bishop as its president, or a priest delegated by him for this task, and a proportionate number of deacons. This organization should not be remiss in maintaining the necessary links with the other diocesan organizations.

The Bishops should regulate the life and activity of this organization by the issuance of appropriate norms.

Married deacons 81.   In addition to the usual permanent formation offered to deacons, special courses and initiatives should be arranged for those deacons who are married. These courses should involve, where opportune, their wives and families. However, they must always be careful to maintain the essential distinction of roles and the clear independence of the ministry.

Other initiatives 82.   Deacons should always be appreciative of all those initiatives for the ongoing formation of the clergy promoted by Conferences of bishops or various dioceses — spiritual retreats, conferences, study days, conventions, theological and pastoral courses. They should avail themselves of such initiatives especially when they concern their own ministry of evangelization, worship and loving service.

The Sovereign Pontiff, Pope John Paul II, has approved this present Directory and ordered its publication.

Rome, at the Office of the Congregations, 22 February 1998, Feast of the Chair of Peter.

DARÍO Card. CASTRILLÓN HOYOS
Prefect

✠ CSABA TERNYÁK
*Titular Archbishop of Eminenziana
Secretary*

PRAYER
TO THE BLESSED VIRGIN MARY

MARY,

Who as teacher of faith, by your obedience to the word of God, has co-operated in a remarkable way with the work of redemption, make the ministry of deacons effective by teaching them to hear the Word and to proclaim it faithfully.

MARY,

Teacher of charity, who by your total openness to God's call, has co-operated in bringing to birth all the Church's faithful, make the ministry and the life of deacons fruitful by teaching them to give themselves totally to the service of the People of God.

MARY,

Teacher of prayer, who through your maternal intercession has supported and helped the Church from her beginnings, make deacons always attentive to the needs of the faithful by teaching them to come to know the value of prayer.

MARY,

Teacher of humility, by constantly knowing yourself to be the servant of the Lord you were filled with the Holy Spirit, make deacons docile instruments in Christ's work of redemption by teaching them the greatness of being the least of all.

MARY,

Teacher of that service which is hidden, who by your everyday and ordinary life filled with love, knew how to co-operate with the salvific plan of God in an exemplary fashion, make deacons good and faithful servants, by teaching them the joy of serving the Church with an ardent love.

Amen